Chekhov In Yalta

(Featuring a Rare and Delightful Visit
by the Moscow Art Theatre)

by
John Driver and Jeffrey Haddow

A SAMUEL FRENCH ACTING EDITION

FOUNDED 1830

New York Hollywood London Toronto

SAMUELFRENCH.COM

IMPORTANT BILLING AND
CREDIT REQUIREMENTS

CHEKHOV IN YALTA was first presented by the Center Theatre Group at the Mark Taper Forum (Gordon Davidson, Artistic Director) in Los Angeles, California on May 24, 1981. It was directed by Ellis Rabb and Gordon Davidson; the scenery was by Douglas W. Schmidt; the costumes were by John Conklin; the lighting was by Martin Aronstein; the original music was by Catherine MacDonald; the fight and dance choreography was by Anthony De Longis. The cast was as follows:

Fyokla................................ Lois Foraker

Anton Pavlovich Chekhov........... Robin Gammell

Maxim Gorky........................ Keene Curtis

Ivan Alexeivich Bunin .... James R. Winker

Masha Chekhov .... Marian Mercer

Olga Leonardova Knipper .... Penny Fuller

Vladimir Nemirovich-Danchenko........ Dana Elcar

Lilina Stanislavski.................... Andra Akers

Luzhki .... Michael Bond

Moskvin............................ Jeffrey Combs

Konstantin Sergeievich Stanislavski... Rene Auberjonois

AUTHORS' NOTE

CHEKHOV IN YALTA may be performed in two acts as written, or may be broken into three acts if this better serves your particular needs.

Even two language experts will differ as to the pronunciation of the Russian names, places, and terms herein. What matters most is that your chosen pronunciations remain consistant throughout your production.

This play is *not* meant to be a parody of Chekhov's plays. Nor is it meant to be a lugubrious dirge. What seems to work best is a happy balance of comedy and drama. This at times may seem like walking a tightrope, but by approaching the piece from the point of view of emotional truth, a stylistic unity can be maintained.

CAST

MASHA CHEKHOV — *30's. Anton's unmarried sister and housekeeper.*

FYOKLA.— *21. Chekhov's maid.*

ANTON PAVLOVICH CHEKHOV — *40. Writer and doctor.*

MAXIM GORKY — *30. Writer of the people. Living in Yalta to treat his consumption.*

IVAN ALEXEIVICH BUNIN — *31. Popular writer of aristocratic descent. Summering in Yalta.*

OLGA LEONARDOVNA KNIPPER — *30's. Leading lady of the Moscow Art Theatre.*

VLADIMIR NEMIROVICH-DANCHENKO — *39. Co-director and business manager of the Moscow Art Theatre.*

LUZHKI — *Mid-thirties. Fat, sentimental actor of the Moscow Art Theatre.*

MOSKVIN — *Late twenties. Young, acrobatic character man with the Moscow Art Theatre.*

LILINA STANISLAVSKI — *31. A delicate beauty and wife of Stanislavski. Ingenue and costume designer for the Moscow Art Theatre.*

KONSTANTIN SERGEIEVICH STANISLAVSKI — *37. Co-director and artistic force behind the Moscow Art Theatre.*

ACT I, SCENE 1
Anton Chekhov's villa in Yalta, April, 1900.

ACT I, SCENE 2
The same, the next day.

ACT II
The same, two days later.

CHEKHOV IN YALTA

ACT I
Scene 1

*Lights up on the patio terrace of ANTON CHEKHOV'S villa in
Yalta. Downstage Left, a path leads off toward the sea.
Upstage Left is a stone wall beyond which is a Tartar
cemetery. Stage Right, a walkway skirts the side of the villa
leading off Upstage towards the front of the house. Farther
Right can be seen the edge of a sub-tropical forest bordered by
a well-tended row of acacia trees. The rear facade of the
three-story villa dominates the Upstage area. Two entrances
lead from the patio into the house, one small entrance Stage
Right to the kitchen, and one larger double-door arrange-
ment opening into the parlor. On the terrace is a grouping of
wicker furniture — armchairs, sofa, table — Downstage
left is a small gazebo. It is spring. Morning fog covers the
ground. In the distance can be heard the sound of the sea. A
boat whistle blows.*

*MASHA CHEKHOV appears at a second floor window in
a frumpy housedress. She is a plain, hard-working woman
who has devoted much of her life to looking after her brother's
welfare. Looking off to the right, she becomes very
excited.*

9

MASHA. Fyokla! *(She disappears into the house, still yelling.)* Fyokla, get up! He's coming. Up, up, up, up, up! *(Brandishing a broom, she chases Fyokla, the maid, an unselfconsciously voluptuous creature.)* Come on, come on, he's here. Get the samovar.

FYOKLA. *(going into the kitchen)* Tired.

MASHA. *(Sweeping FYOKLA out of the house with the broom.)* Trollop! Strumpet! You should have thought of that last night.

FYOKLA. *(from kitchen)* Last night, miss?

MASHA. *(wiping the dew from the patio furniture)* I saw you sneaking back from the cemetery.

FYOKLA. *(returning with the samovar)* No, miss.

(Sound of carriage approaching.)

MASHA. I watched you climb in through the window.

FYOKLA. *(setting down the samovar)* It wasn't me.

MASHA. Liar! Go get his blanket. *(She shoos FYOKLA back into the house.)*

(ANTON CHEKHOV enters with medical bag. He is forty, but looks much older. He is in a highly energized state common to sufferers of consumption, a state which, though giving the appearance of robust health, is in reality an exhilaration brought on by fever.)

CHEKHOV. What a night!

MASHA. *(wiping off the chair)* Antosha, come, sit. Rest.

CHEKHOV. *(pacing around)* But it was worth it. On the

way back here I saw a curious thing. A drunken ice merchant had run his cart into a ditch. He was sitting on a block of ice, sobbing and tearing his hair out. I can probably turn that into a very amusing story. *(MASHA is trying to lead him to the chair without success. FYOKLA enters with blanket.)* Fyokla, there's a crate in the droshky. Fetch it here, will you?

MASHA. *(Snatching the blanket and sending FYOKLA off. Leading CHEKHOV to chair.)* You ought to be ashamed of yourself. Out all night in your condition. Why does God give me such a brother? *(She finally gets him seated, places the blanket over his legs.)* Where were you?

CHEKHOV. At Tolstoy's estate. It's all very generous of him to go about preaching independence of spirit to his peasants, but it's only succeeded in making them afraid to ask for medical help when they need it.

(FYOKLA enters with a crate containing a live chicken.)

MASHA. What is that?

CHEKHOV. My fee. These people have no money. *(FYOKLA takes the chicken to the kitchen.)* I delivered a baby, set a few limbs, pulled a tooth ... Then for the rest of the night, I had to sit and listen to Tolstoy expound on the simplicity of the Russian soul. *(He pops up out of the chair.)* God, I'm hungry. Must be the sea air. Fog is burning off. The weather is going to be perfect today. I'm so bored here, unimaginably bored. *(He coughs as he takes a cigar from his pocket and pats his jacket for matches.)* Masha, do you have some matches?

MASHA. *(disapprovingly, indicating cigar)* Anton ...

CHEKHOV. It was a gift from Tolstoy.

MASHA. Please, you promised. *(He reluctantly hands the cigar to her. She leads him off once more to the chair.)* Antosha, I know you're having one of your good days, but *you* know very well all this exhilaration is not natural. Your cheeks are flushed with fever. It'll catch up with you. It always does. *(FYOKLA Has fallen asleep over the samovar. CHEKHOV takes out his notebook and begins writing as MASHA takes a bottle of medicine and spoon from her apron. Seeing FYOKLA, MASHA bops her on the head with the spoon.)*

FYOKLA. Ow!

CHEKHOV. Semyon! That's a good name for an ice merchant.

MASHA. *(reaching for the notebook)* No writing. Just rest.

CHEKHOV. *(jerking notebook back angrily)* No, Masha, no! Now just go away and leave me alone.

MASHA. *(Stops CHEKHOV's speech by shoving a spoonful of medicine in his mouth.)* I'd appreciate it, Anton, if you would use some of your boundless energy to speak to Fyokla. She was in the cemetery with her corporal again last night.

(MASHA exits into house. FYOKLA serves tea, starts to go.)

CHEKHOV. Fyokla, come here. What were you and that soldier doing in the cemetery last night?

FYOKLA. We were ... picking mushrooms, sir.

CHEKHOV. You know how much that upsets my sister.

FYOKLA. Picking mushrooms, sir?

CHEKHOV. Masha tells me your nocturnal harvesting companion is known throughout the district as a notorious cad. Now, believe me, I understand the temptations and the joys of your midnight trysts...

FYOKLA. Thank you, sir.

CHEKHOV. But if you cause a scandal, Masha will make all of our lives a living hell. Do you understand?

FYOKLA. I think so, sir.

CHEKHOV. That will be all, Fyokla. By the way, I'm looking forward to mushrooms for lunch.

FYOKLA. Yes, sir, I'll go to the market and buy some. *(She exits.)*

CHEKHOV. Hm. The body of a goddess, the brain of a flea. *(He takes out notebook again. Writes.)*

(MASHA enters, listens as she cleans.)

CHEKHOV. Where was I? Oh, yes, Semyon, the ice merchant. One day, while he's making his rounds, he receives word that his nagging, gluttonous wife has choked to death on a piece of black bread. That's good. That's funny. *(MASHA shakes her head and exits. CHEKHOV sips tea, grimaces.)* Feh! Medicinal tea. Ah, Yalta, Yalta, my warm Siberia!

(Enter MAXIM GORKY, tall, dark, Tartar features, flowing black hair, dressed in peasant blouse, breeches, and riding boots. With him is IVAN BUNIN, elegant, aristocratic. They are carrying on a mock duel with fishing poles.)

GORKY. Parasite!

BUNIN. Hypocrite!

GORKY. Tsarist pig!

BUNIN. Crass peasant!

CHEKHOV. Masha! Bunin and Gorky are here.

BUNIN. *(Scores a hit.)* Aha! A hit!

GORKY. *(Grabs BUNIN's pole and snaps it in two.)* Touché!

BUNIN. You're a barbarian, Gorky.

CHEKHOV. Masha! How can you let three of the world's greatest writers languish from thirst?

GORKY. *(Swipes the notebook away from CHEKHOV.)* Ah, ah, none of that today.

CHEKHOV. What are you talking about?

BUNIN. Gorky's just formed a writers' union.

GORKY. And today we're on strike.

BUNIN. Like all strikes, Anton, it's merely an excuse to go fishing. And to that end... *(handing CHEKHOV a sack)* ... we've come bearing a gift.

CHEKHOV. Worms. How nice.

GORKY. *(quietly)* Come here and look, but keep talking. *(He crosses to wall.)*

BUNIN. They're fat ones too, Anton.

GORKY. From the cemetery. You can find all sorts of crawling things in the cemetery. *(He indicates that two men are behind the wall.)*

CHEKHOV. So? A couple of gravediggers playing cards.

GORKY. They're secret police.

CHEKHOV. *(as they all peek over the wall)* Nonsense.

GORKY. Look at the one on the right. See the bulge in his blouse? That's an oak truncheon filled with lead.

They say he's killed five men with it.

CHEKHOV. They're simple gravediggers, Maxim. You flatter yourself terribly to think the Tsar's men are watching you from behind every tree.

BUNIN. It's the leaflets. He's writing those leaflets again.

GORKY. They don't dare arrest *me*. The public outcry would be too great.

BUNIN. I can hear the crowds now, yelling "Give us Barrabas!"

GORKY. They've heard us.

(FYOKLA enters and serves tea.)

CHEKHOV. Fyokla, have you seen my fishing pole?

FYOKLA. No, sir.

CHEKHOV. Well, find it, and bring it here, please. Maybe this bait will change my luck.

BUNIN. *(Drinks tea, spits it out.)* Ptooey! Yeccchh.

GORKY. Wonderful tea. My grandmother made tea like this.

FYOKLA. I'll make a new pot.

BUNIN. Oh, don't waste it. I can always use it to clean my shotgun.

CHEKHOV. My fishing pole, Fyokla.

FYOKLA. Yes, sir. *(FYOKLA exits. GORKY begins winding his fly. BUNIN repairs his pole.)*

(MASHA comes out. She's taken off her apron and primped a bit.)

MASHA. Good morning, Ivan, Maxim.

BUNIN and GORKY. Masha.

MASHA. *(Smiling at BUNIN; notices shirt.)* Ivan, what happened to your shirt?

BUNIN. I was attacked by an animal.

MASHA. Well, it can be mended. The tear is on the seam.

(FYOKLA enters with fishing pole. Hands it to CHEKHOV.)

FYOKLA. It was on the piano. *(She exits.)*

MASHA. *(Swipes the fishing pole from CHEKHOV.)* Oh, no, you're too weak to go fishing. *(She's about to exit when BUNIN stops her.)*

BUNIN. Masha, surely a woman capable of such affection, such devotion, should be able to recognize the enormous theraputic value of fishing.

MASHA. I don't know...

BUNIN. The soothing music of the babbling brook, the healing vapors of the pine glade...

MASHA. No, Ivan, what if he catches a fish and gets all excited?

BUNIN. Why should today be any different?

MASHA. *(weakening)* But he was up all night.

GORKY. *(to CHEKHOV)* You were?

CHEKHOV. Yes, I was at Tolstoy's.

BUNIN. Oho, that's enough to exhaust a plowhorse. Take a nap. We'll come back later.

CHEKHOV. No, no, don't go. Masha, pack a basket for us to take with us.

BUNIN. *(to MASHA, delicately taking fishing pole)* Please.

MASHA. Well...

BUNIN. Thank you, Masha. *(She smiles at him and exits into the house. BUNIN hands pole to CHEKHOV in triumph. The men continue tying flies.)*

CHEKHOV. You won't believe what Tolstoy came up with this time. He said he couldn't tolerate Shakespeare's plays.

BUNIN. What conceit!

GORKY. Only Tolstoy could get away with that.

CHEKHOV. Then he said my plays were even worse. *(imitating Tolstoy)* "Nothing happens in your plays, Anton." *(silence)* He must have seen Stanislavski's production of *Seagull.* All those pauses. *(pause)* I nearly fell asleep myself.

GORKY. Have you finished *The Three Sisters?*

CHEKHOV. Yes.

BUNIN and GORKY. Congratulations.

BUNIN. Has the Moscow Art read it yet? *(silence)* You *have* sent it to the Moscow Art...

CHEKHOV. No ... I've sent it to the Imperial Thaetre. *(pause)* I know what you're thinking. Everyone says Stanislavski is a genius, but you saw what he did to my *Seagull.* Granted it was supposed to be night, but the lights were so dim the audience could hardly see the stage. And that constant cacophony of nightingales, hoofbeats, creaking gates, rustling leaves, strange noises in the forest. And his brilliant idea of a plague of imaginary insects. All through the second act the players were slapping themselves so loudly you couldn't hear what they were saying. If I gave them the new play, I'd have to have someone make an entrance in every scene just to say, "What a marvelous place! There are no mosquitoes."

BUNIN. But the Moscow Art is in Sebastopol. They'll be here tomorrow. What will you tell them?

CHEKHOV. I'll say it's not finished.

BUNIN. Better not tell Knipper till after she's been to the beach house, eh. Anton?

GORKY. Olga Knipper?

BUNIN. You should see them together.

GORKY. Serious?

BUNIN. Methinks fatal. *(GORKY hums the "Wedding March.")*

CHEKHOV. Nonsense. I have escaped the dreaded snare of matrimony for 40 years. My religion is to remain single.

BUNIN. Has the Temple of the Beach House been made ready for Knipper?

GORKY. One actress moves out, another moves in. I hope at least you changed the sheets.

CHEKHOV. Not a word about Komisarevskaya to anyone.

BUNIN. The secret of social success unveiled! Become a consumptive playwright and beautiful actresses will tug at your breeches.

GORKY. Nothing fires a woman's loins like a coughing writer.

CHEKHOV. Pleasure always has its price, my friends. After Komisarevskaya left I was an invalid for a week. Thank God she had an engagement to star in an Ibsen play in Rostov. Ach, Ibsen, now there's an atrocious playwright.

GORKY. Nothing happens in his plays.

CHEKHOV. Why does Stanislavski insist on doing my plays the same way he does Ibsen's? I write comedies. *(BUNIN whistles a little tune. Awkward silence.)*

(Sound of the sea.)

GORKY. Wind has shifted to the south. You can hear the breakers.

CHEKHOV. Ivan, how would you describe the sea?

BUNIN. The sea ... The sea. A wall of tears ... fallen from the eyes of the Mother Of Life. A restless opalescent tabletop ... reflecting the depths of cosmic sorrow.

CHEKHOV. Maxim?

GORKY. The enormous black sea appears calm. But beneath that serene facade lies a monstrous denizen of discontent. It is an embroyo, never having seen the light, never having breathed the air of freedom. For centuries it has gathered size and substance. It is waiting, waiting for the right moment to burst from its womb and cut the night fog with the fiery blue sword of Justice.

BUNIN. Thank God. For a second there I thought you were going to get political.

CHEKHOV. I was looking over some of my old copybooks, and I came across this quote. In my opinion it is the most perfect description of the sea ever written. "The sea is huge." *(GORKY and BUNIN assent. Awe.)* I always carry it with me as a reminder to write simply.

(Enter OLGA KNIPPER, strong-willed, vital, uniquely attractive, a commanding leading lady who is both self-centered and ambitious.)

OLGA. Dr. Chekhov, I presume?

CHEKHOV. Olga.

OLGA. *(She kisses him on both cheeks and sweeps around the terrace.)* Oh, this is paradise. Palms, hibiscus, bouganvilla...

CHEKHOV. I planted all the acacias myself. *(OLGA is standing before BUNIN.)*

BUNIN. *(bowing)* Madamoiselle Knipper.

OLGA. Monsieur Bunin, how are you?

GORKY. *(Approaches her.)* Olga Leonardovna, may I say you were wonderful as Arkadina in *Seagull.*

OLGA. A man of exquisite taste.

CHEKHOV. Oh, I'm sorry, you two haven't met, have you? Olga Knipper, Maxim Gorky.

OLGA. *(She offers her hand to GORKY. He shakes it vigorously.)* I'm dazzled. Surrounded by literary lights.

(MASHA enters.)

MASHA. Olga! You're a day early!

OLGA. Masha! *(She embraces MASHA.)* I'm sorry, dear, we tried to telephone but you know how those machines are.

CHEKHOV. You'll be staying the night, then?

(Enter VLADIMIR NEMIROVICH-DANCHENKO, dapper, bearded managing director of the Moscow Art. He is carrying a small parcel.)

NEMIROVICH. I'm afraid not. We'll be rehearsing till all hours this evening but I promise you, after the performance tomorrow night your villa will become the Pension Moscow Art.

CHEKHOV. Nemirovich!

NEMIROVICH. Anton Pavlovich, how are you?

CHEKHOV. Fine, fine. Ivan Bunin, Maxim Gorky, this is Vladimir Nemirovich-Danchenko, director of the Moscow Art Theatre.

NEMIROVICH. Co-director, please.

CHEKHOV. Ah, yes. With ... what's his name.

NEMIROVICH. Masha, how nice to see you again. *(OLGA takes the parcel from NEMIROVICH, hands it to MASHA and whispers something in her ear.)*

MASHA. Ah! Fyokla! *(She exits into the house.)*

NEMIROVICH. Gorky, why didn't you come backstage to see us while you were in Moscow?

GORKY. I was under surveillance. Still am as a matter of fact. I didn't want to get you involved in that.

NEMIROVICH. Ah, yes. I've heard it said you attract police like baklava draws flies.

CHEKHOV. When did you leave Moscow?

NEMIROVICH. On the twelfth.

GORKY. Then you were there when it happened. The students must have marched right past your theatre.

CHEKHOV. What are you talking about?

NEMIROVICH. You didn't hear about it? Last Tuesday. People were killed. Students and Cossacks fighting in the streets.

OLGA. It was terrifying. Several students were trampled to death. I saw a Cossack cut off a boy's hand.

NEMIROVICH. We had to cancel rehearsal.

CHEKHOV. There was no mention of it in the newspapers.

GORKY. *(contemptuously)* The newspapers.

NEMIROVICH. The gutters ran with blood.

OLGA. At the station we saw them loading coffins onto the mail train.

GORKY. They'll pay for this. For each one killed, a thousand will rise to take his place.

BUNIN. Even in Russia, there can't be that many suicidal fools.

OLGA. Anton, last week we saw Chaliapin in *Boris Godunov.* Bravo Chaliapin! *(No-one is listening. OLGA heads for the house. To herself, in her lowest register.)* Bravo, Chaliapin! *(She exits into the house.)*

GORKY. Wait till the workers start joining the students.

NEMIROVICH. God help us if that happens.

CHEKHOV. It won't happen.

GORKY. It will, Anton. And in our lifetime.

CHEKHOV. But to burn, to tear down ... No, give the people books, teach them to read, make them healthy.

GORKY. No, the solution is quick and simple — chop off the head of the Imperial Eagle!

BUNIN. *(glancing toward the wall)* For God sake, Gorky, keep your voice down.

(OLGA enters carrying a tray of oysters. She is followed by FYOKLA and MASHA.)

OLGA. Anton!

CHEKHOV. Oysters! Where did they come from?

OLGA. I brought them packed in ice.

CHEKHOV. Ah, Olga, you know so well how to make

me happy. You all must be hungry.

NEMIROVICH. Ravenous.

GORKY. How many dead?

OLGA. Can't we please talk about something else?

BUNIN. For Maxim there is no other subject.

GORKY. Everything is political. Even these oysters. A metaphor for the masses.

BUNIN. Perfect. After all, they are lazy and stupid. Day in, day out, lying passively on the bottom doing nothing.

GORKY. Not at all. They're working, always working, silently producing pearls to hang about the necks of bourgeois swine.

OLGA. But Maxim, what about the oysters that don't produce pearls?

CHEKHOV. They, my dear actress, make excellent appetizers. *(Everyone digs into the oysters.)*

NEMIROVICH. So, Anton, how is the new play coming? *(ANTON, chewing, cannot speak.)*

MASHA. He's finally finished it, thank God. *(CHEKHOV chokes, the choking turning into a serious coughing fit. MASHA rushes to him.)*

OLGA. Are you all right?

CHEKHOV. I'm fine. You see? I've stopped.

MASHA. Come on, Antosha. You need to lie down.

CHEKHOV. Nonsense. I'm perfectly well. I must have choked on a pearl.

OLGA. I'll help you upstairs.

MASHA. I can manage myself, thank you. *(MASHA leads CHEKHOV into house.)*

BUNIN. He was worn out. We should have left him

alone. *(GORKY coughs.)* Maybe we should put you in bed, too.

NEMIROVICH. Good lord, does everyone in Yalta have consumption?

BUNIN. Almost everyone. But you needn't worry. It isn't contagious.

NEMIROVICH. I know that. *You* certainly look healthy enough.

BUNIN. Yes, and its kept me out of all the better social clubs. Well, Maxim, shall we?

GORKY. By all means. *(to others)* Until tomorrow. *(They start to leave.)*

(FYOKLA runs in with jar full of brown liquid.)

FYOKLA. Wait, Ivan Alexeivich! *(Hands BUNIN the jar.)*

BUNIN. What's this?

FYOKLA. It's tea. For your shotgun. *(BUNIN and GORKY laugh and exit. FYOKLA exits. OLGA takes a cigarette from a case in her handbag.)*

NEMIROVICH. *(He lights it for her.)* We must have that play.

OLGA. Your concern for his health is touching.

NEMIROVICH. I am concerned. I am very concerned. It is up to you to make sure he continues to be our playwright.

OLGA. Why, Vladimir? Why are you pressuring me like this? You can't use me like you did in former times. I'm not your adoring student anymore.

NEMIROVICH. Sometimes I miss those former times.

OLGA. How's your wife?

NEMIROVICH. As promiscuous as possible at her age.

OLGA. You two have so much in common. But this time you're going too far.

NEMIROVICH. What are you talking about?

OLGA. Your current assault on Madame Stanislavski is a mistake.

NEMIROVICH. I have no intention...

OLGA. You have every intention. The longing looks across the room, the significant smiles, the well-chosen words of extravagant praise. Don't forget, you played that game with me, but I'm strong, Lilina is not.

NEMIROVICH. You have an over-active imagination.

OLGA. Do I? Stanislavski may not be able to see anything beyond the footlights, but you can't fool me. Lilina is terribly unsettled right now about her marriage and her work. She pours valerian drops into her tea and still she can't sleep.

NEMIROVICH. Does Anton love you?

OLGA. Don't change the subject.

NEMIROVICH. Does he?

OLGA. That's none of your business.

NEMIROVICH. Believe me, it is.

OLGA. Why should it be? If you want my help, you'd better tell me.

NEMIROVICH. All right. This is in strictest confidence, Olga. Last month we could barely afford to heat the theatre. If we don't have a financial success this season, and that means a new Chekhov play, the doors of the Moscow Art will close forever.

(MASHA enters and hovers silently in the background.)

OLGA. Dear God...

NEMIROVICH. You see now. We didn't come to Yalta for our health.

OLGA. My relationship with Anton has nothing to do with the Moscow Art.

NEMIROVICH. Oh, please, don't play the fool with me. What actress wouldn't want to be Madame Chekhov. *(MASHA drops something. They turn and see her.)* Ah, Masha, may I use your telephone?

MASHA. You can try.

NEMIROVICH. How is Anton Pavlovich?

MASHA. A little better now, thank you. *(NEMIROVICH exits.)* I'm so worried. He seems much worse.

OLGA. Oh, you're exaggerating.

MASHA. He had an attack! He coughed up blood. Consumption runs in the family, you know. Our brother Nikolai died of it.

OLGA. Oh, yes, Anton was fond of him, wasn't he?

MASHA. Yes. Poor Nikolai. He was a wonderful artist. His illustrations for Anton's stories were so sensitive. He was quite young. *(pause)* Olga, can I ask you a favor?

OLGA. Of course, dear.

MASHA. Well ... What do you think of Bunin?

OLGA. He's witty, charming...

MASHA. Oh, yes, he is, he is. Well, you see, Ivan and I have become friends. We talk, we have long conversations. But the subject is always Anton. To him, I'm only Chekhov's spinster sister.

OLGA. A spinster! Don't be ridiculous, Masha. You're

younger than I am.

MASHA. I am?

OLGA. Perhaps not.

MASHA. But you have charm, Olga. You know how to talk to men. *(hopefully)* You could even talk to Bunin about me.

OLGA. Oh, Masha, I have no talent as a go-between, and I hardly know the man.

MASHA. Please...

OLGA. And if he's not interested in you?

MASHA. Then I'll forget all about him.

OLGA. Well...

MASHA. Thank you, thank you. Oh, Olga, Olga, what would I do without you.

OLGA. All right, I'll do it. But from now on, you must be completely honest with me.

MASHA. I've always been honest with you.

OLGA. Not when it comes to Anton.

MASHA. I just don't want you to be hurt, Olya. He's not as good as you think he is.

OLGA. What does that mean?

MASHA. Nothing.

OLGA. You see? You're holding back.

MASHA. Less than a month ago, Komisarevskaya was here.

OLGA. What?

MASHA. For three days.

OLGA. And how many nights?

MASHA. He calls her his Russian Duse.

OLGA. His Russian Duse!

MASHA. I shouldn't have told you! I shouldn't have.

OLGA. I will talk to Bunin, and I'll be as honest with you as you've been with me. Komisarevskaya, that scheming bitch.

MASHA. I'm sorry I told you.

OLGA. Why? It's the truth, isn't it?

MASHA. But it's so unfair. Oh, Olya, how can we go on living with this hopelessness? *(They cry and embrace.)*

(CHEKHOV enters.)

CHEKHOV. Did Stanislavski direct this scene?

MASHA. What are you doing down here? Go back to bed. I sent for Dr. Altschuler. He'll be here soon.

CHEKHOV. What do I need a doctor for? I am a doctor. I take my pulse. *(Can't find it.)* Strange, it was here yesterday. Ah, there it is. And when I look at Olga, it beats twice as fast. I'm healthy as a bull. Masha, bring my cigars.

MASHA. I will not let you smoke while I'm in this house.

CHEKHOV. Fine, bring me my cigars and leave. *(MASHA storms out.)* Olga *(They kiss passionately.)* Mmm. Can't do that in a letter.

OLGA. You've tried, Anton.

CHEKHOV. The things we've done on paper.

OLGA. You've lost weight, Antosha.

CHEKHOV. Ach, it's nothing. But you, look at you. How is Moscow?

OLGA. The same. Oh, there's a new restaurant. Last Thursday after the performance we went there with that critic Piontov, you know, the one you call...

CHEKHOV. Pontifikov.

OLGA. He's really quite amusing. There he sat, holding court, praising the delicate subtleties of Chekhov's plays while caviar dripped from his beard and his fingers groped my knees under the table.

CHEKHOV. Filthy pig.

OLGA. Oh, we had such fun. Why didn't you come to Moscow as you promised?

CHEKHOV. Ah, Dr. Altschuler, that Prussian tyrant, forbade me to travel.

OLGA. Why? Are you so sick, Anton? You can trust me.

CHEKHOV. But I do, you know I do, my little Russian Bernhardt.

OLGA. Bernhardt? Why not Duse?

CHEKHOV. Duse? Oh no, Duse is a tragic figure.

(FYOKLA enters with humidor.)

FYOKLA. Your cigars, sir.

CHEKHOV. *(Tries to open the humidor. It's locked.)* Fyokla, it's locked. Where's the key?

FYOKLA. Masha has it.

CHEKHOV. Well, tell Masha to bring it to me.

FYOKLA. She's not here. She went to market *(Starts out, comes back.)* Oh, here's your matches. *(She exits.)*

CHEKHOV. Could I borrow one of your hairpins? *(OLGA gives him one.)* I've built a little house on the beach.

OLGA. Oh?

CHEKHOV. Very private. Two rooms, the sound of the sea, and it's particularly romantic when moonlight streams through the bedroom window.

OLGA. Is that where you made love to Komisarevs-kaya?

CHEKHOV. The devil made this lock.

OLGA. I said is that where you made love to Kom-isarevskaya?

CHEKHOV. What a part I've written for you in *The Three Sisters.*

OLGA. The mistress of a famous writer?

CHEKHOV. That wouldn't be quite accurate, would it? Not yet. *(pause)* Ah, Knipschütz, you're taking this whole matter much too seriously.

OLGA. And you're not taking me seriously at all. Love is no joke, Anton, people shoot themselves over it. *(pause)* Tell me about the part.

CHEKHOV. It's only the best woman's role I've ever written.

OLGA. We *will* do a reading while we're here, won't we?

CHEKHOV. Olga, if some other theatre were to do this play, would you consider doing the role?

OLGA. Anton! How could you even *think* of such a thing. What ingratitude! It's an outrage.

CHEKHOV. You don't have to decide right now.

OLGA. Do you have a contract?

CHEKHOV. I believe soon.

OLGA. Why?

CHEKHOV. You know why.

OLGA. Stanislavski. *(pause)* You've never understood him, have you, Anton? He's bold, he's an experi-menter.

CHEKHOV. My plays are not laboratory animals.

OLGA. But you can't deny that as an actor there's no one to compare with the man. Such a force, such a presence...

CHEKHOV. Such an idiot. He can't even remember his lines.

OLGA. Antosha, please, tell me you'll reconsider. *(He coughs.)* Your cough is timed so conveniently.

CHEKHOV. *(coughing more)* Sounds quite natural, doesn't it?

OLGA. *(concerned now)* Perhaps you should be in a sanitorium.

CHEKHOV. Yalta is the biggest open-air sanitorium in Russia. I'm receiving treatment with every breath I take. *(more coughs)*

OLGA. *(becoming a bit alarmed)* Is there anything I can do?

CHEKHOV. There is one thing. Dr. Altschuler has recommended the beach-house cure.

OLGA. Hmm, I wonder how many actresses have fallen for that? *(CHEKHOV holds up four fingers, five. OLGA playfully slaps his hand down.)*

CHEKHOV. *(taking out notebook)* What was that you said before? "Love is no laughing matter, people shoot themselves over it." I can't use that. It sounds like fiction.

OLGA. But it's not fiction.

CHEKHOV. *(writing)* "Sounds like fiction, but it's not fiction." Good.

OLGA. Am I just another one of your short stories?

CHEKHOV. I don't know. We haven't gotten past the first few pages, have we?

OLGA. You've never written a novel, have you
Anton?

(NEMIROVICH enters.)

NEMIROVICH. Olga, we must be off. Good-bye Anton Pavolovich.

CHEKHOV. Good-bye. Oh, Nemirovich, do you happen to have a cigar?

NEMIROVICH. Shouldn't smoke, Anton, bad for the
lungs. *(He exits.)*

OLGA. Well, until tomorrow.

CHEKHOV. Until tomorrow night. There'll be a full
moon.

OLGA. Dreamer. *(She exits.)*

CHEKHOV. *(returning to notebook)* Semyon the ice man.
Where was I? Damn! Olga makes me nervous. *(He renews
his assault on the humidor lock.)* Even when she's not here,
she invades my privacy. I can't get any work done. *(pause)*
The clinics never helped Nikolai. He slept all day. His
face became flushed and bloated. His clothes hung
about his emaciated body and flapped in the wind. His
fingers didn't even have the strength to hold a pencil. He
had to be bathed. Humph. And I can't even bear to be
seen without a tie. *(The lock springs open. He takes out a cigar
and lights it.)* No, I don't have time to write a novel.

(Lights fade.)

END OF SCENE 1

ACT I
Scene 2

*The following night. Sound of a door bell. Shouts. Group heard
singing Russian folk song accompanied by gramophone carried in by one of the actors. OLGA, BUNIN, GORKY,
NEMIROVICH, and FYOKLA burst onto the terrace carrying bottles of wine and vodka. With them are LUZKHI, a
fat sentimental actor, MOSKVIN, a young, acrobatic
character man, and LILINA, the delicately beautiful wife of
STANISLAVSKI. MASHA enters from the kitchen with
tray of medicines. Dancing and singing continue, featuring
a beautiful solo by OLGA, and ending in a spectacular
Cossack dance by MOSKVIN. Applause. Silence. Crickets.*

MASHA. *(having gotten caught up in the merriment, now picks
up tray and heads for house)* Fyokla, bring some glasses.
(FYOKLA exits.)

OLGA. How is Anton Pavlovich?

LUZHKI. Did he like us?

MASHA. He's resting well. He apologizes for having
left early and says he'll be down later. Excuse me. *(She
starts for the house.)*

OLGA. I'll go with you. *(MASHA and OLGA exit into
the house.)*

NEMIROVICH. Where's Stanislavski?

LILINA. Still at the theatre signing programs for young girls.

LUZHKI. I was mobbed once in Petersburg — But they were creditors.

BUNIN. Would somebody please tell me why all the actors were crying during the second act?

MOSKVIN. We were drunk.

LILINA. Just before the curtain went up some prankster put vodka in the samovar.

LUZHKI. It was the best performance of *Vanya* we ever did. *(MOSKVIN mimes disagreement.)* Where are those glasses?

(FYOKLA enters with glasses.)

NEMIROVICH. It's one o'clock already.

EVERYONE. No. It couldn't be ...*(etc.)*

LILINA. Moscow seems a million miles away.

LUZHKI. *(crying)* Ah, Moscow, Moscow.

MOSKVIN. Warm night.

LILINA. It was terribly hot onstage.

BUNIN. At least there's a cool breeze tonight.

NEMIROVICH. Why discuss it? There's nothing to be done about the weather.

LUZHKI. It's in God's hands.

GORKY. Why should that be?

LILINA. Why?

GORKY. Why should God control the weather and man have nothing whatsoever to say about it? When there's a storm is it God who gets shipwrecked? Is it God who freezes to death catching fish to feed His starving family?

God doesn't depend on the wheat, God's skin doesn't blister in the desert. It's quite clear. God forfeited His rights by His supreme indifference. *(NEMIROVICH is asleep.)*

BUNIN. Gorky, you've whipped us all into a frenzy. *(MOSKVIN burlesques a fit of frenzy culminating in a backflip.)*

LUZHKI. Fyokla, you have some fish in the house? Maybe a little herring? I'm hungry.

GORKY. Fish would be nice.

LUZHKI. *(draining the last drop of vodka)* The vodka's finished. Anybody want more?

LILINA. You do.

BUNIN. *(starting toward the house)* I know where Anton Pavlovich keeps his private stock.

GORKY. Anyone else drinking bordeaux? *(GORKY and BUNIN exit into house.)*

LUZHKI. I can't drink another drop.

EVERYONE. What?

LUZHKI. Unless we have music. Moskvin, did you see? Anton Pavlovich has a piano inside. Come play.

LILINA. Luzhki, Moskvin's tired. What do you think he is, a trained monkey? *(MOSKVIN exits imitating monkey. LUZHKI shrugs and follows. LILINA gazes at NEMIROVICH. LILINA starts toward house.)*

(Singing and piano are heard.)

NEMIROVICH. *(catching LILINA's arm)* My blood boils for you.

LILINA. Why, Vladimir, why this sudden ardor after all these years?

NEMIROVICH. Feel my forehead, I'm on fire.

(OLGA enters.)

NEMIROVICH. You see, if the hat comes down to the eyebrows, the face is obscured. Other than that, your designs for the Hauptmann play are exquisite.

LILINA. Why, thank you, Vladimir Ivanovich.

OLGA. Can't you two talk about anything but the theatre?

NEMIROVICH. Is Anton Pavlovich all right?

OLGA. Yes, he's all right, no thanks to Masha.

NEMIROVICH. Ladies, if you'll excuse me. *(He exits. LILINA takes out her needlepoint, begins to work.)*

OLGA. Masha wouldn't even let me stay in the room. She's hovering over him like a mother hen. If you confine a man to a sickroom he'll become a sick man. He's no invalid when he's with me. *(LILINA breaks down.)* Lilina, what's the matter? It's Nemirovich, isn't it? That snake.

LILINA. No. It's everything. Everything. What will happen to us? The government is spying on the theatre, everyone is spouting high-minded words about revolution. I don't understand. And that riot last week. I keep seeing those bodies in the street.

OLGA. The other day there was no bread in the shops.

LILINA. Where is it all leading, Olga? The ground is moving under our feet. Last month a group of drunken workers from Kostya's factory stood under our bedroom window and shouted horrible obscenities. I was terrified.

Especially now that Kostya sleeps in the study.

OLGA. Oh?

LILINA. For six months now.

OLGA. It is another woman?

LILINA. Yes, the theatre. The theatre is his mistress. He's slipping away from me, Olga. His mind never leaves the stage. My presence does nothing but irritate him. I suppose I remind him that he's mortal. He wants me to stop acting.

OLGA. He said that?

LILINA. It's the subtext of everything he says. You've seen how he abuses me with his criticism.

OLGA. He abuses everyone.

LILINA. You don't have to go home with him.

OLGA. Lilina, look, you've sewn your ring into the pattern.

LILINA. *(ripping the cloth violently)* What's wrong with me? I can't even act anymore. There's a hollowness now, and the audience can feel it.

OLGA. You're imagining that.

LILINA. Well, there's one thing I'm not imagining. Kostya sees me as an annoying piece of baggage that won't stay home in the closet. Look at me. There are dark circles under my eyes. How much longer will I be able to play ingenue roles?

OLGA. Lilina, what are you talking about? When we're onstage together, I work twice as hard, and still everyone is watching you. Nemirovich has surely been taken by your charms.

LILINA. Yes. Oh, Olga, I'm tempted, but it's impossible.

OLGA. Careful, darling. He has an uncanny talent for sniffing out unsatisfied women.

(MASHA enters.)

MASHA. He looks like a little boy when he sleeps. So peaceful. He needs me, Olga.

OLGA. I think this may be a good time to have that little chat with Bunin.

MASHA. Oh, yes, yes!

NEMIROVICH. *(poking head in)* Come join us, ladies. How can we dance without you? Lilina?

LILINA. I'd love to. *(She exits with NEMIROVICH.)*

OLGA. Go on, Masha. Tell Bunin I want to have a word with him.

MASHA. Don't you think tomorrow would be better? What if he rejects me? I couldn't take it. I'll kill myself. I'll enter a convent.

OLGA. Very well, I won't talk to him.

MASHA. All right, all right. *(She exits.)*

OLGA. Poor Masha. What a cruel fate to be such a nonentity. *(Finds CHEKHOV's hat on bench.)* I wish I could put this on and know your thoughts. *(talking to the hat)* What do you want from me? Oh, God, I'm tired of casual affairs. Please don't let this be another one.

(Laughter is heard from the house. BUNIN enters.)

BUNIN. Olga Leonardovna, is something wrong?

OLGA. What do you mean?

BUNIN. Well, Gorky was in the middle of a humorous

anecdote when Masha woke me and said you wanted to see me. She was pale as chalk. What is it?

OLGA. Oh, it's nothing, really, Ivan Alexeivich. I simply wanted to have a little chat with you.

BUNIN. Ah, a chat.

OLGA. Actually, I need your advice.

BUNIN. Well, I must warn you, I'm much better at pointless conversation.

OLGA. Forgive me if I don't mention names, but I have a friend who is in love with a certain man.

BUNIN. Ah, a friend.

OLGA. But she's very shy, and she's not sure how this man feels about her.

BUNIN. Why are you telling *me* all this?

OLGA. I value your opinion. You're an astute judge of character. I see that especially in your poetry.

BUNIN. Continue.

OLGA. The man in question is everything a woman could want: good-looking, talented, very intelligent...

BUNIN. And your friend?

OLGA. She would make an excellent wife. In fact, they would make an ideal couple, if the man loved my friend as much as she loves him.

BUNIN. Is this mysterious man a writer?

OLGA. I think you understand who we're talking about.

BUNIN. Oh, yes, it's quite obvious, isn't it? But I don't believe the woman loves the man as deeply as you say.

OLGA. Take my word for it, she does, and she must know the man's true feelings for her. What do you think?

BUNIN. I think you're absolutely wrong for him.

OLGA. What?

BUNIN. If Anton marries you, he'll be committing suicide.

OLGA. Oh my God!

BUNIN. You know how sick he is. In his condition he's an easy mark for a beautiful woman like you. If he tries to keep up with your hyper-active Moscow social life, he'll be dead before the honeymoon's over.

OLGA. How vicious!

BUNIN. No, just frank. You keep him out revelling till four in the morning, you encourage him to drink, you buy him cigars...

OLGA. What crimes! When he's with me in Moscow, he's invigorated. He enjoys life.

BUNIN. And we bring him back to Yalta on a stretcher coughing up blood. Don't you see? This is hardly the time in Anton's life for you or anyone else. *(OLGA laughs.)* Did I say something funny?

OLGA. The man in my little story was not Anton.

BUNIN. You said he was a writer.

OLGA. That's right.

BUNIN. *(astonished)* Gorky?

OLGA. No.

BUNIN. *(surprise)* Ahhh! *(pause)* Don't tell me you're in love with me.

OLGA. The woman is Masha.

BUNIN. Masha! *(Laughs. Stops laughing.)* Masha.

(Sound from the house. CHEKHOV has come downstairs. Enter CHEKHOV followed by NEMIROVICH, LILINA, LUZHKI, MOSKVIN, GORKY and MASHA.)

NEMIROVICH. What didn't you like about the production?

MASHA. *(to OLGA, whispering)* What did he say?

OLGA. Later.

LUZHKI. It was me. It was me. I put the vodka in the samovar. I ruined everything. *(He eats a herring.)* Anton, you know these provincials. All they want is slapstick. *(MOSKVIN does raspberry, pratfall, picks himself up by the collar.)*

GORKY. What can you expect from an audience of merchants?

LUZHKI. They didn't even cry.

CHEKHOV. They're not supposed to cry.

LUZHKI. They're not? *(to NEMIROVICH)* They're not? But it's so moving when Vanya tries to shoot the professor.

CHEKHOV. It's not moving. It's funny.

LUZHKI. That's funny?

CHEKHOV. The play is practically a vaudeville. How could you misinterpret it so? I wrote it all down. And that's another thing, why do you improvise?

NEMIROVICH. Don't be too hard on Stanislavski. Learning lines is not his forte.

CHEKHOV. But tonight he replaced one of my monologues with a speech from *Hedda Gabler.*

NEMIROVICH. He did?

(FYOKLA enters with tray of hors d'oeuvres. She trips, falls with a crash, and several people help her pick up the food. KONSTANTINE SERGEIEVICH STANISLAVSKI, flamboyant co-director of the Moscow Art Theatre, sweeps into the scene. No one notices.

He goes out, comes back in again, and clears his throat.)

STANISLAVSKI. Hello, everyone. I'm here.

CHEKHOV. Ah, Konstantine Sergeievich, we were just talking about you.

STANISLAVSKI. Nothing bad I hope. *(Chuckles. Sits in CHEKHOV's chair.)* The show was rather good tonight, I thought.

LILINA. *(pause)* Isn't the garden lovely, Kostya?

OLGA. Anton Pavlovich planted all the acacias himself.

STANISLAVSKI. *(dejected, to CHEKHOV)* You didn't like it. You left early.

CHEKHOV. I loved it. Really, it was wonderful. I liked the acting in particular. *(STANISLAVSKI puffs up with pride.)* Especially Moskvin. *(MOSKVIN acts shy.)* But it wasn't my play.

STANISLAVSKI. What do you mean? We did our best to present the reality of your text. We used real food, real tea, we created the atmosphere of a real country dacha with the sounds of birds, cows, crickets...

CHEKHOV. The stage is not a barnyard. The stage is not life. It is the quintessence of life.

STANISLAVSKI. I spoke to a critic after the show. He loved it. I remember his exact words. He said ... uh ... well, he was impressed with the, let me see, yes, "the twilight mood of melancholy."

CHEKHOV. What melancholy? There isn't even one death.

STANISLAVSKI. Anton, you seem to be unaware of the depth of your gift.

CHEKHOV. When I write, I know exactly what I'm doing. *Uncle Vanya* is a comedy.

STANISLAVSKI. Certainly it has it's comic moments, yes, but on the whole anyone would have to agree, it's a tragedy.

LUZHKI. Why don't we take a vote?

STANISLAVSKI. When I'm wrong, I'm the first to admit it. *(MOSKVIN whistles.)*

LUZHKI. How many think *Uncle Vanya* is a comedy? *(Nobody. Then CHEKHOV, then GORKY raise their hands.)*

GORKY. An artist must always be supported in his own opinions about his work ... even when he's wrong.

NEMIROVICH. Anton, try to look at it as a practical solution to a creative problem. Most playgoers come to the theatre to cry.

CHEKHOV. Sheep. Let them cry at weddings and funerals.

NEMIROVICH. And if they cry, they tell their friends, and their friends buy tickets. No tears, no Moscow Art.

CHEKHOV. But surely they want to laugh, too.

STANISLAVSKI. There's too much truth in your plays.

CHEKHOV. Sometimes the truth is comical. Even ridiculous.

STANISLAVSKI. Then why don't they laugh at it?

CHEKHOV. Because you make them cry.

LUZHKI. It's my fault. It's all my fault.

STANISLAVSKI. Your plays touch people. They move people. They strike a responsive chord, Anton Pavlovich. I remember when we were in rehearsal for our first production of *Seagull.* Quite frankly, I have to admit it, I,

Konstantin Stanislavski, did not understand the play. I thought, my God, the audience will be throwing cabbages at us by the end of the first act. It was only the encouragement and the prophetic genius of Nemirovich-Danchenko that prevented me from losing all hope. You see, our very survival that first season depended on the reception of that play. The theatre had spent its last ruble on the production. Our noble experiment to change the course of theatrical history was in danger of being dashed on the reefs of financial ruin. And, as if that weren't enough, Masha, who loves you with all of her generous heart, forgive me for telling your little secret, Masha, sent us letters, telegrams, and finally, two days before our opening night, she came to the theatre in person. She spoke quietly through her sobs. You were ill, she cried, very ill, and then this dear, sensitive creature actually fell to her knees before the entire company and begged us, implored us, beseeched us not to open the play. She said, and these were her exact words, "If this play fails, uh ... *(MOSKVIN makes motion of hammer and nail.)* ... it will drive the final nail into Anton's coffin." But it was too late. We had to go on. Opening night before the curtain went up we were terrified. Upon this one cast of the die depended not only the fate of the Moscow Art Theatre but perhaps the very life of our revered Chekhov as well. The boards of the stage had become a gallows and we the executioners. Everything seemed to be against us. Olga Leonardovna was running a high fever, my poor Lilina was groggy from too many valerian drops. I personally was so overcome with tension that I had to sit with my back to the audience in order to stop my leg from shaking. Fortunately, I had staged myself with my back to the audience.

LUZHKI. A great innovation.

STANISLAVSKI. Thank you. In the first five minutes, three sound cues were missed. I could see Masha in her box, clutching at her handkerchief. Nemirovich was pacing up and down the lobby. He couldn't even bring himself to watch the performance. The audience was cool, uncertain. We played without thinking, as if we were possessed. The first act ended, the curtain fell, and there was total silence. We knew we were lost. Olga fainted, I sank to my bench, Luzkhi broke down, Lilina ran offstage, and Moskvin squatted with his head between his legs ... Then, suddenly, there was an explosion of applause! They cheered, they screamed, they stamped their feet. The curtain rose and caught us in our ridiculous positions. We took call after call. They shouted again and again for the author. Our theatre was saved, and our own Anton Chekhov was baptized as Russia's greatest living playwright! ... Where is he? *(CHEKHOV has exited quietly during the speech.)* Did I say something wrong? *(sits)* What does he have against me? He doesn't like me as an actor, he doesn't like me as a director, I don't even think he likes me as a person.

MASHA. I'm sorry, Konstantin. Antosha simply cannot tolerate praise, particularly in public. *(She exits. GORKY, already drunk, pulls cork from a wine bottle with loud pop. GORKY and LILINA exit into house. OLGA starts to leave.)*

LUZHKI. Olya, could I borrow five rubles till Friday? These new cuts in our salaries are killing me.

OLGA. Get it from Moskvin. *(MOSKVIN pulls his pockets*

inside out and makes a sad face.)

LUZHKI. Him? He'd let his grandmother eat hail-stones.

OLGA. You already owe me twenty-six rubles. Isn't that right, Moskvin? *(MOSKVIN nods.)*

BUNIN. Here, Luzhki. Five rubles?

LUZHKI. Oh. I couldn't. I hardly know you. Actually I need ten if you can spare it. *(BUNIN, LUZHKI and MOSKVIN exit. OLGA makes sure no one is watching, and exits along the Down-Left path. FYOKLA is cleaning and watching STANISLAVSKI.)*

(Piano can be heard from within.)

FYOKLA. Pardon me, I thought your speech was ... was...

STANISLAVSKI. Brilliant?

FYOKLA. Yes, brilliant! Thank you, thank you. *(She runs off, embarrassed.)*

STANISLAVSKI. Nice girl, who is she? *(to NEMIROVICH)* Vladimir, what does Anton Pavlovich expect of me? You know, I don't think he understands his own plays. With any other director, *Uncle Vanya* would be inaccessible to the public.

NEMIROVICH. It's the best thing you've done.

STANISLAVSKI. Mark my words, Chekhov will not be remembered. Now, Potapenko or Griboyedov — those are names that will echo down the halls of history.

(Hear piano, under.)

STANISLAVSKI. He steals from Ibsen.

NEMIROVICH. Oh, Kostya, he doesn't steal.

STANISLAVSKI. He's boring. His characters do nothing but chase each other's wives.

(LILINA enters.)

LILINA. Kostya, it's late.

STANISLAVSKI. We should make a new policy. From now on, we only do plays by deceased writers. They don't make such a fuss when you improve on their work.

LILINA. Kostya, I'm going to bed. Good night Vladimir.

NEMIROVICH. Good night, Lilina. *(LILINA exits.)*

STANISLAVSKI. We need that new play of his. What's it called? *The Three Brothers?*

NEMIROVICH. Sisters.

STANISLAVSKI. I hope there's a good man's role in it. Where's Lilina?

(Enter BUNIN and GORKY, both drunk.)

GORKY. I'm surrounded and suffocated by enemies of the *(hic)* people.

STANISLAVSKI. Ah, Gorky, at last I have the opportunity to tell you how much I admire your work.

NEMIROVICH. Yes, Maxim, have you ever considered writing for the theatre?

GORKY. As a matter of fact, I am working on a play.

STANISLAVSKI. Wonderful! What's it about?

GORKY. The absurdity of life in Russia. Starvation,

proverty, humiliation, disease.

STANISLAVSKI. We really need a comedy.

NEMIROVICH. We need anything you write, Maxim.

GORKY. I'll only give it to you on one condition. It has to be free.

NEMIROVICH. Free?

GORKY. No admission charge.

STANISLAVSKI. We do have very cheap seats.

GORKY. Free.

NEMIROVICH. Well, we'd love to do that of course, but there are costs involved in running a theatre: scenery, costumes, props...

STANISLAVSKI. Sound effects.

NEMIROVICH. We have to heat the theatre.

GORKY. You think you're artists? You're businessmen. You, Konstantin Sergeievich, you own a factory, your father was a rich merchant. And you, Nemirovich-Danchenko, married to a wealthy baroness, what do you know about the misery of a peasant's existence?

BUNIN. I've heard they often seek relief from their terrible lives by fornicating with chickens.

GORKY. Bunin, Bunin, Bunin. The Bunins have always had their tongues securely up the Tsar's anus. *(Makes move to attack BUNIN, falls over chair.)* Ummmgah!

NEMIROVICH. *(helping him up)* Perhaps after a good night's rest we can discuss the proposition.

GORKY. Don't touch me, dung-face.

BUNIN. Remarkable command of the language.

GORKY. I feel ... I feel ... *(Runs off.)*

(Sound of retching.)

GORKY. *(off)* Jesus, oh God... *(retch)*

BUNIN. There. That's the opening monologue from his play.

STANISLAVSKI. Bunin, you should join our company. You'd be a fine actor, I can tell.

BUNIN. Never. I'm far too humble to be an actor.

GORKY. *(stumbling back on)* The storm is coming! It's coming while you sit in your salons talking about ideals. Hah! Ideals. Peasants know nothing of ideals. The earth is their only reality. It is their mother and their curse. They scratch at it all their lives, gaining nothing, burying their children beside their parents, passing over the land like ghosts or cattle. Oh, I'm so tired ... *(He passes out.)*

BUNIN. *(Takes off his jacket. Lays it over GORKY.)* Look at him, the voice of the People, the model peasant in his rustic blouse of Japanese silk, his Italian leather boots with silver buckles ... *(Takes bottle from GORKY's hand.)* And see what he drinks? Only the finest bordeaux. Do you know how much rent he pays on his villa? It's not difficult to be a peasant when you have money. Yet it's strange how I envy this man. I can only mouth flowery platitudes to a race of dinosaurs, while he proclaims the dark future.

(LUZKHI and MOSKVIN enter singing. They stop, swaying.)

LUZHKI. Look, Moskvin, the moon! And, there, Venus is rising.

GORKY. *(Coming to. Singing.)*
I TOOK HOME A LADY NAMED VENUS
AND ASSURED HER THAT NO ONE HAD SEEN US.

WHILE I STROKED HER FAIR SKIN,
HER MOTHER WALKED IN,
JUST AS VENUS WAS KISSING MY...
(Passes out. Everyone, tensed for the word, relaxes.)

STANISLAVSKI. When I was young, I played in an operetta called *The Queen of the Night.* And in it there was a glorious speech about the moon. I still remember it. "Oh, Moon ... " *(pause)* Well ...

BUNIN. I'll lug the guts into the neighbor room.

STANISLAVSKI. Macbeth. I love Macbeth.

MOSKVIN. Hamlet.

STANISLAVSKI. Moskvin, you talk too much.

LUZHKI. You watch that tongue of yours, Moskvin. Come on, it's late. *(MOSKVIN and LUZKHI follow BUNIN and GORKY into the house.)*

(FYOKLA enters, cleaning.)

NEMIROVICH. I think I'll retire for the night. What about you Konstantin?

STANISLAVSKI. No, it's such a pleasant evening.

NEMIROVICH. Ah, good night then.

STANISLAVSKI. See you in the morning. *(NEMIROVICH exits.)* Ma, me, mi, mo, mu. Ma, me, mi, mo, mu. Oh, Moon... *(Begins to weep. FYOKLA comes closer, also begins to cry. STANISLAVSKI sees her.)* Why are you crying, girl?

FYOKLA. Because you're crying, sir.

STANISLAVSKI. No, no, I'm just practicing.

FYOKLA. Practicing? You mean you were acting?

STANISLAVSKI. Ah, no, it was more than acting. I was actually experiencing great sorrow.

FYOKLA. I believed you.

STANISLAVSKI. And see, now I'm cheerful. I'm speaking to you as if nothing happened. What's your name, girl?

FYOKLA. Fyokla, sir.

STANISLAVSKI. Don't be deceived, my dear Fyokla. Acting is not as easy as I make it appear to be. Years of labor and sacrifice must be invested in the theatre, and even then, without the God-given gift of Talent, an actor can never be more than a mere gramophone mechanically reproducing the speech and gestures of others.

FYOKLA. How can a person tell if she has a gift?

STANISLAVSKI. Whenever a young, would-be actress asks me that question, I say to myself, how can I best evoke this person's artistic potential. How?

FYOKLA. (blankly) I don't know.

STANISLAVSKI. Oh, you're perfect. Absolutely unburdened by any knowledge whatsoever. Let me give you a simple exercise. Stand there. Now, imagine yourself arriving home after the most rapturous afternoon of your life. The rich young man you love has just proposed to you. (moving table) Now, this table will represent a table, and this napkin will be a telegram informing you that your father has just died. The door is upstage center.

FYOKLA. Where?

STANISLAVSKI. There. You come in, see the telegram, read it, and react. Do you understand?

FYOKLA. Yes, yes.

STANISLAVSKI. Good, proceed.

FYOKLA. (Enters laughing, melodramatic gestures, sees telegram, does long take, picks it up, drops pose.) Shouldn't you write the message on this?

STANISLAVSKI. No, no, no, use your ... How do I explain this. There's a kind of magic about the theatre. You must act as *if*...

FYOKLA. Magic? If?

STANISLAVSKI. *(He's made a brilliant discovery.)* Yes, the magic "if!"

FYOKLA. I don't understand.

STANISLAVSKI. Pretend.

FYOKLA. *(staring at the napkin)* Oh. But, sir, I can't read.

STANISLAVSKI. Pretend you can read. Do it again. And don't move your arms about like that. *(FYOKLA exits.)* The Magic If. What a concept!

FYOKLA. *(Enters, does the same scene with arms stiffly at sides, gets to telegram.)* Can I move my arms to pick up the telegram?

STANISLAVSKI. Yes.

FYOKLA. *(Picks up telegram.)* Oh, Papa. *(Swoons mechanically, looks at STANISLAVSKI expectantly.)*

STANISLAVSKI. In all my twenty years in the theatre, I have never seen anything so intolerably bad.

FYOKLA. *(crying)* I'm a gramophone! I'm a gramophone!

STANISLAVSKI. Now that's the kind of reaction you should have had to the telegram. *(taking FYOKLA by the shoulders)* Remember this feeling. Etch it in your memory. *(FYOKLA plays up to STANISLAVSKI.)* You see? Acting is not a child's game. It is a monumental task. The actor must work with all the perserverence of a grunting, sweating fieldhand.

MASHA. *(offstage)* Fyokla!

FYOKLA. Teach me more. Please, teach me more, right now!

STANISLAVSKI. Shhh. It's late. Your mistress calls. We mustn't wake everyone. Another time.

FYOKLA. No, now.

STANISLAVSKI. I've already given you far too much for one evening. Why you could work on that little scene for ... two years.

MASHA. *(offstage)* Fyokla!

FYOKLA. Coming. *(Halfway to door, stops, stamps foot.)* No, I'm going to practice my acting. I'll be in the cemetery under the willow tree if you want to give me more exercises. *(exits)*

STANISLAVSKI. Ah, she's hopeless.

(LILINA enters.)

LILINA. Kostya, please come to bed.

STANISLAVSKI. Ah, Lilina. Would you bring me my make-up case? It's just inside the door. *(LILINA exits.)* The willow tree. Hmm.

LILINA. *(Returns with kit.)* Kostya. It'll be morning soon.

STANISLAVSKI. *(Kneads putty, sets up mirror on bench.)* You must be tired. Go to bed.

LILINA. I want you to come to bed with me, Kostya.

STANISLAVSKI. Are you blind? Can't you see I'm building a nose?

LILINA. Kostya ...

STANISLAVSKI. Kostya, Kostya, Kostya! Leave me alone.

LILINA. This is important.

STANISLAVSKI. Important? This nose is the single most important external detail of my Dr. Astrov. *(looking for something in kit)*

LILINA. I've got to talk to you.

STANISLAVSKI. It's the wrong time to talk now.

LILINA. It's always the wrong time to talk.

STANISLAVSKI. We talk all the time.

LILINA. No, we don't. You talk. I listen.

STANISLAVSKI. You left the top off the clown white again. Details, my dear, details. Attention to detail is everything.

LILINA. I need attention, Kostya. Maybe you don't feel it, but our marriage is falling apart, and I'm afraid.

STANISLAVSKI. Rubbish! It's a phase, like the moon. It'll pass. Lilina, how many times do I have to tell you ... the spirit gum goes to the right of the brushes, and the face powder should always be set alongside the dry rouge. Is that so difficult to remember?

LILINA. Why, no. I'll rearrange it right now. *(She picks up the kit and dashes it to the floor.)*

STANISLAVSKI. Have you gone mad, woman? It's taken me twelve years to assemble that kit. Pick it up immediately and put everything back ... in the correct order! *(Picks up mirror, putty, stalks toward house, changes mind, goes off toward cemetery. For LILINA, anger turns to resignation. She stoops to reassemble kit.)*

(NEMIROVICH enters. He begins to help her. He takes rouge, makes up LILINA's lips, and kisses her. He stands, tries to lead her.)

NEMIROVICH. Come to my room. *(She resists. He puts a hand down her robe. She begins to swoon.)*

(MASHA enters.)

MASHA. Oh, I was looking for Fyokla.

NEMIROVICH. Haven't seen her.

MASHA. Lilina, would you like to come have some tea?

LILINA. No.

NEMIROVICH. Good night, Masha. *(MASHA exits.)* Come to my room.

LILINA. No, go away. *(Embraces him. Pushes him away. Runs towards the cemetery. Stops. Nemirovich calmly walks to her, puts his arm around her. He leads her into house.)*

(Sound of sea. CHEKHOV and OLGA enter.)

OLGA. I can't imagine what happened to it.

CHEKHOV. Did you look in the bushes? I might have thrown it out the window in the heat of the moment.

OLGA. Oh, no, what if someone finds it? We'd better go back.

CHEKHOV. Oh, here it is! *(Opens jacket. He is wearing OLGA's corset.)*

OLGA. Anton, take that off.

CHEKHOV. Why, Olga, what sort of man do you think I am?

OLGA. A shameless rake. *(chukles)* I never thought I'd see it. The great Chekhov without his starched collar.

CHEKHOV. Did I cut such a ridiculous figure?

OLGA. Yes, but it was heavenly. I was beginning to think that collar was a permanent part of your body.

CHEKHOV. And you, my dear actress, always in such control on the stage. It was a great pleasure to see you so...

OLGA. ...Eager to nibble at your flesh?

CHEKHOV. Olga! *(Moment of silent affection.)*

OLGA. Do you love me?

CHEKHOV. My little cantaloupe...

OLGA. Cantaloupe, melon, pumpkin. Antosha, I think I deserve to know what's under this pile of fruits and vegetables.

CHEKHOV. Come to Italy with me.

OLGA. Yes, affairs are taken for granted there.

CHEKHOV. You are so perfect for *The Three Sisters.*

OLGA. No, Anton, I can't. I can't go to the Imperial Theatre. The Moscow Art is like a family to me. Besides, how would it look? The gossip-mongers from the press are already whispering about us. If I went to Petersburg with your play they'd brand me as Chekhov's whore.

CHEKHOV. What do you care what the press says?

OLGA. They're dragging my name through the mud.

CHEKHOV. You're an actress. Any publicity is good publicity. *(She slaps him.)* The contract from the Imperial Theatre is on its way and I'm going to sign it.

OLGA. Fine ... That tells me quite a lot, your choosing to slap me back with that piece of news. How little you must think of me! The Imperial Theatre. Oh, I'm sure the production will be very grand. You'll reap a fortune, won't you, Anton? Never mind that the evening will be under-rehearsed and over-acted, and that your play will be reduced to a melodramatic costume parade. *(beat)* It'll mean the end of the Moscow Art ... Yes, without your play we're lost. Well, I shouldn't have told you that, but I suppose it doesn't mean anything to you anyway ... It's maddening. I'm sure I'm losing a choice role, a real plum. But my ambition and the company's finances have nothing to do with *us. (pause)* Oh, you can be such a fool, Anton. The first time we met after rehearsal in that freezing hall, I knew you'd already fallen in love with me. Why can't you admit your feelings?

CHEKHOV. Love is a fantasy. A tragic dream.

OLGA. Well, then, here are some cold facts for you. I am not Komisarevskaya. I don't bargain with my flesh for a part in a play. I gave myself to you for one reason. I love you. I love you deeply. But I must be your equal, nothing less. Set a date, Anton, or get another mistress. *(She exits.)*

CHEKHOV. *(Takes humidor from hiding place, it is empty.)* Oh, Masha.

(STANISLAVSKI enters with nose.)

STANISLAVSKI. Anton Pavlovich, what do you think of the new Dr. Astrov?

CHEKHOV. God forbid he should sneeze. Join me for a drink, Konstantin?

STANISLAVSKI. *(taking nose off and putting it carefully on the bench)* Yes, I do believe I ... *(Sees make-up kit.)* Damn! *(Gets down on his knees, and begins putting kit back in order. CHEKHOV gives STANISLAVSKI drink.)* Thank you.

CHEKHOV. Do you have a cigar, Kostya?

STANISLAVSKI. Yes, yes. *(Hands CHEKHOV cigar.)* Ah, you smoke my brand.

STANISLAVSKI. Yes, Masha gave me a whole box.

CHEKHOV. Hm. Cheers.

STANISLAVSKI. Cheers.

CHEKHOV. Another?

STANISLAVSKI. Please. Such an enchanting night. I took a stroll through the cemetery.

CHEKHOV. *(brushing dirt from STANISLAVSKI's jacket)* Looks like you took a crawl through the cemetery.

STANISLAVSKI. *(lying)* Yes, I tripped over a shovel, fell on a fresh grave.

CHEKHOV. What happened to your make-up?

STANISLAVSKI. Accident. *(CHEKHOV keeps pouring drinks. Stanisvlavski finishes up, snaps case shut.)* Women.

CHEKHOV. So demanding.

STANISLAVSKI. So impulsive.

CHEKHOV. So yielding.

STANISLAVSKI. Yes. To women.

CHEKHOV. What would we do without them?

STANISLAVSKI. Get some work done.

CHEKHOV. Become extinct.

STANISLAVSKI. Ah, memento mori. Isn't it curious how sex and death are so intimately related?

CHEKHOV. Are they? I think that's perverse.

STANISLAVSKI. How can you say that? The greatest literary minds have made the comparison.

CHEKHOV. And now you.

STANISLAVSKI. Who was it said, "Only the religious

need fear death because..."

CHEKHOV. "...they're the only ones who believe in a hereafter."

STANISLAVSKI. Yes! Who said that?

CHEKHOV. I did.

STANISLAVSKI. Ah, yes, of course. *(Beat. CHEKHOV coughs.)*

STANISLAVSKI. Ah, the ocean. I was walking on the beach tonight when suddenly I stopped and stood transfixed by the waves. I was struck by an incredible revelation. Anton, the sea is huge.

CHEKHOV. *(Takes out notebook, rips out page, throws it away.)* One last drink.

STANISLAVSKI. No, thank you.

CHEKHOV. A nightcap.

STANISLAVSKI. Well, in that case ... *(He accepts the drink and sits heavily on the bench.)* Oh, Anton, have I told you about the magic "if?"

CHEKHOV. You're sitting on your nose.

STANISLAVSKI. What? Oh, oh. *(He groans, peeling the flattened nose from the bench.)*

CHEKHOV. What a nice tie you're wearing.

STANISLAVSKI. Hm? Yes, Lilina made it.

CHEKHOV. Nice. I admire your marriage. Not everyone can be as fortunate as you've been with Lilina.

STANISLAVSKI. Ah, but I haven't the slightest doubt that were you and Knipper to wed, your marriage would be every bit as idyllic as my own. *(pause)* Anton, do you know why your plays work better at the Moscow Art than anywhere else?

CHEKHOV. Why?

STANISLAVSKI. Love.

CHEKHOV. Oh, no, not love again.

STANISLAVSKI. Each and every member of our company has a personal devotion to you and your work, Anton, that I guarantee you would not find in any other theatre in Russia. *(beat)* I'm so glad we're having this little chat. Oh, yes, we've had our differences. I know, sometimes I can be a pompous ass.

CHEKHOV. You're absolutely right.

STANISLAVSKI. No, no, don't be kind. I can, I can be. But I want you to know, I do everything in my power to make your plays work.

CHEKHOV. I know. I appreciate it, but you don't have to go to all that trouble.

STANISLAVSKI. Why, if it weren't for you and *The Wild Duck*...

CHEKHOV. *The Seagull.*

STANISLAVSKI. Whoops, wrong bird. *(pause)* We have to work together. After all, if you've got a play but no director, you don't have a play.

CHEKHOV. No play.

STANISLAVSKI. And if you've got a director but no play, you don't have a play.

CHEKHOV. No play.

STANISLAVSKI. We need each other.

CHEKHOV. You're absolutely right.

STANISLAVSKI. I'm so happy you've decided to give the new play to us.

CHEKHOV. I haven't.

STANISLAVSKI. From the bottom of our hearts I thank

we us. *(They get up, unsteadily walk toward house. STANIS-LAVSKI throws his arm around CHEKHOV.)* Anton?

CHEKHOV. What?

STANISLAVSKI. Are you wearing a corset? *(They exit into house.)*

(Morning sounds. Lights fade.)

END OF ACT I

ACT II

Two days later. Sunday morning. Church bells are heard in the distance. Clouds are gathering. OLGA and FYOKLA bustle about setting up for a party.

OLGA. Fyokla, set the plates there and put the silverware in neat rows on the side. *(OLGA sets glasses around the samovar.)*

FYOKLA. Madame Knipper, may I ask you a professional question?

OLGA. Professional?

FYOKLA. Yes. Where did you learn acting?

OLGA. I studied with Nemirovich at his school in Moscow. Oh, I hope it doesn't rain.

FYOKLA. Was he a good teacher?

OLGA. Yes, he's excellent, especially with beginners. Napkins! Go get napkins. *(FYOKLA turns to leave, stops, breaks down.)* Fyokla, what's the matter?

FYOKLA. Oh, nothing. Just practicing. *(She exits.)*

(MASHA enters on LUZHKI's arm.)

MASHA. Olga, look. I didn't have to go to church alone today.

LUZHKI. It was my pleasure, Masha. You saved my soul. If not for you, I would've had nothing to put in the offering plate. I'll pay you back, though. Oh, I wish we weren't leaving today.

MASHA. *(seeing table settings)* Olga! You used Mother's lace. I told you not to start without me. And the good crystal.

OLGA. What good is it if you never use it?

MASHA. Change it immediately. Fyokla!

(FYOKLA enters.)

MASHA. Bring the linen tablecloth. *(FYOKLA exits.)*

OLGA. There's no time.

LUZHKI. Where's the food? Kneeling makes me hungry. Maybe in the kitchen? *(LUZHKI exits.)*

MASHA. And why have you set it like a buffet instead of a proper dinner?

OLGA. I arranged things so they could be carried into the house quickly if it rains.

MASHA. It won't rain.

(FYOKLA comes back with the linen.)

OLGA. Take that back inside and bring the napkins. *(FYOKLA exits.)*

MASHA. That lace will be ruined if it rains.

OLGA. You said it wouldn't rain.

MASHA. *(Pours herself a drink.)* Olga, we have a way of doing things here. There is a time and place for everything in this house. Using fine lace outdoors in a buffet setting is vulgar. I don't want people to think I have no taste. Oh, it's not your fault. You couldn't have known the lace was being saved for an occasion.

OLGA. This *is* an occasion.

MASHA. A *special* occasion.

OLGA. And what would you consider special enough? Anton's wedding, perhaps?

(NEMIROVICH enters.)

NEMIROVICH. Ah, Masha, you're back. Where's Luzhki?

MASHA. In the kitchen.

NEMIROVICH. I should have known. What a lovely setting.

OLGA. How much time do we have?

NEMIROVICH. I told Moskvin and Gorky to keep Anton fishing at least until noon.

(LILINA enters.)

LILINA. Can I help?

NEMIROVICH. Good morning, Lilina. Did you sleep well?

LILINA. Very well, thank *you*.

NEMIROVICH. How's Kostya's speech coming along?

LILINA. I don't know. He's getting into make-up right now.

NEMIROVICH. Make-up for a speech? God help us. Where is he?

LILINA. Upstairs.

NEMIROVICH. Ladies, if you'll excuse me. *(He exits.)*

(FYOKLA enters.)

FYOKLA. Ma, me, mi, mo, mu *(She exits.)*

LILINA. Masha, I'm sorry I didn't wake up early enough to go to services with you.

MASHA. Well, you were probably exhausted. *(She exits.)*

OLGA. She's upset because her house has been invaded by libertines.

LILINA. She wouldn't complain if she were one of them.

OLGA. Hmmm. Quite a change has come over you in the last two days, Lilina. Infidelity seems to agree with you.

LILINA. Olga, someone might hear.

OLGA. Lord knows, I'm not criticizing you.

LILINA. I do feel marvelous. I keep waiting for the guilt to come, but so far...

OLGA. I know that euphoria, Lilina. I know it well. But don't forget, you're on the road. It's easy to live dangerously when you're away from home.

LILINA. I don't intend to bring any of it back to Moscow if that's what you mean.

OLGA. Nemirovich may not feel the same way. You're walking a tightrope, darling. If you lose your balance, you'll bring the theatre down on all of us.

LILINA. My, aren't we quick to moralize. No proposal again last night?

(Enter STANISLAVSKI and NEMIROVICH.)

NEMIROVICH. I tell you, Konstantin, he'll walk out.

STANISLAVSKI. We've been on very good terms lately.

(FYOKLA enters with hors d'oeuvres.)

OLGA. Not now. If you bring them out now, they'll attract flies! *(OLGA takes the hors d'oeuvres back to the kitchen.)*

NEMIROVICH. This party is a tribute to him. It's our last chance to get that play.

STANISLAVSKI. Exactly, leave it to me.

MASHA. *(offstage)* Fyokla, the pieroshki! I need you. *(FYOKLA exits.)*

STANISLAVSKI. Don't worry, Vladimir. This will be very funny. A tour de force.

NEMIROVICH. Anton won't like it. When it comes to his plays, he has no sense of humor.

LILINA. You see? That's exactly what I said.

STANISLAVSKI. What do you know? *(to NEMIROVICH)* I tell you my presentation is clever enough to amuse even the stoical Chekhov.

LILINA. It's silly.

STANISLAVSKI. It's what?

NEMIROVICH. You'll make a complete fool of yourself.

STANISLAVSKI. Such a coward. Look at the fear in his eyes. Always so afraid to offend. In this case, Vladimir, your financial expertise is irrelevant.

NEMIROVICH. Not quite. He almost gave *Uncle Vanya* to the Maly Theatre because of your stupidity. If you insult him again, we'll lose the new play.

STANISLAVSKI. You're wrong, you're wrong, you're wrong, you're wrong!

LILINA. Don't be such a baby, Kostya.

STANISLAVSKI. This is between Nemirovich and myself,
Lilina. Leave us alone.

LILINA. But Kostya...

STANISLAVSKI. I told you to keep out of this.

NEMIROVICH. It's too risky.

STANISLAVSKI. Everything's too risky for you. Why in
Christ's name did you ever get into the theatre?

LILINA. Don't swear.

NEMIROVICH. I absolutely forbid you to do this.

STANISLAVSKI. How dare you forbid me to do anything!

LILINA. Please, Kostya, I think Vladimir is right this
time.

STANISLAVSKI. This matter involves creative judge-
ment, Lilina, something I've found to be notably lacking
in your mind.

NEMIROVICH. He'll walk out, I'm telling you.

STANISLAVSKI. Very well, when Chekhov comes in,
we'll all get down on our knees and kiss his feet.

LILINA. Vladimir, when he's in this state, there's no use
arguing with him.

STANISLAVSKI. Is this the way you support me?

LILINA. It's for your own good.

STANISLAVSKI. I should strike you, Lilina, but I want
you to see that I still have some measure of self-control.
However, I'm warning you. Don't say another word. Just
go to the kitchen with the other women. That's where you
belong. *(LILINA starts to leave.)* You can't stop me,
Vladimir, I'm going to do it.

NEMIROVICH. Fine. You're the one who'll destroy the
theatre. The responsibility will be on your shoulders.

LILINA. Vladimir and I are lovers. *(NEMIROVICH freezes.)*

STANISLAVSKI. *(turns)* What?

LILINA. Vladimir and I are lovers.

NEMIROVICH. Oh, Lilina.

STANISLAVSKI. Cuckold?

NEMIROVICH. It's not true. Lilina, what a cruel joke!

STANISLAVSKI. I've done nothing to deserve this.

LILINA. What have I done? Oh my God, what have I done?

NEMIROVICH. Why did you tell him?

STANISLAVSKI. Why did you do it?

LILINA. I only wanted to get your attention. *(She exits. NEMIROVICH starts out.)*

STANISLAVSKI. Must you go so soon?

NEMIROVICH. *(Sits. Pause.)* Looks like rain.

STANISLAVSKI. Stabbed in the back and the knife twisted. What sort of treacherous fiend are you that you would risk everything we've worked for for these past three years solely for the gratification of your indiscriminate lust?

NEMIROVICH. I'm sorry, I'm sorry. It was ... foolish.

STANISLAVSKI. Sorry? Foolish? The end of the Moscow Art Theatre is no mere folly. You have deprived the Twentieth Century of its most significant theatrical institution. Our relationship is severed. Utterly.

NEMIROVICH. *(pause)* You can have my wife. Then we'll be even.

STANISLAVSKI. Bastard. You try to run a theatre without me. Oh, you have a head for figures and a nose for new plays, but you have no artistic spine. You'll founder on the rocks of mediocrity.

NEMIROVICH. Hah! I'd like to see *you* manage a company. After one production, your actors would be reduced to eating roots and leaves.

STANISLAVSKI. Oh, how you flatter yourself. Your duties could be better performed by a monkey with an abacus.

NEMIROVICH. You fool. I've written some of the most popular plays we've done.

STANISLAVSKI. Popular, that's the key word, isn't it? Drawing room excrement.

(MOSKVIN runs in gesturing frantically, pointing off stage)

MOSKVIN. Konstantin Sergeievich! ...

STANISLAVSKI. Not now.

MOSKVIN. Vladimir Ivanovich! ...

NEMIROVICH. Later, Moskvin. It was I who brought Anton Chekhov to the Moscow Art.

STANISLAVSKI. Oh, you have my undying gratitude for that.

MOSKVIN. Please, listen.

NEMIROVICH. Quiet!

STANISLAVSKI. Can't you see we're busy? *(MOSKVIN gives up, goes into the house.)*

NEMIROVICH. I do all the work while you wallow shamelessly in undeserved applause.

STANISLAVSKI. I'll never speak to you again.

NEMIROVICH. This could be a blessing in disguise.

STANISLAVSKI. Contemptible worm!

NEMIROVICH. Pretentious windbag!

STANISLAVSKI. You're nothing but a clerk! A drab clerk!

NEMIROVICH. And you're a selfish, pig-headed pea-cock! I see Lilina was right about you. You haven't mentioned her once. Ah, but I'm sure all these emotions you're cataloguing will be very useful on the stage. *(STANISLAVSKI swings at NEMIROVICH. NEMIROVICH ducks and grabs a chair — holding it out in front of him like a lion-tamer.)*

(CHEKHOV enters with GORKY and BUNIN holding fishing poles.)

CHEKHOV. *(Sees STANISLAVSKI and NEMIROVICH.)* What's all this?

STANISLAVSKI. *(awkward pause)* Surprise!

(OLGA, MASHA, LUZHKI, FYOKLA, MOSKVIN, and LILINA enter carrying trays of food and glasses.)

EVERYONE. Surprise!

STANISLAVSKI. The chair will be fine just there, Vladimir. I'll be waiting for your introduction. *(Exits hurriedly collaring MOSKVIN on the way out.)* Why didn't you say something?

NEMIROVICH. Uhm Anton Pavlovich. We of the Moscow Art are proud and happy to show our appreciation for your invaluable contribution to our theatre by throwing this little party for you. *(MASHA carries a tray of glasses filled with champagne. Everyone takes one. Applause.)*

CHEKHOV. I can't tell you how sorry I am that you've

gone to all this trouble. *(general disappointment)* But I promise you, no matter how unbearable the praise becomes, I will try with all my heart to avoid leaving.

EVERYONE. Hurrah!

MOSKVIN. *(raising glass)* To Chekhov!

BUNIN. To Chekhov! A truly civilized human being. *(scattered "Na zdorovie" 's)*

GORKY. To Chekhov! A man who knows better than any other playwright in Russia, how to treat chronic hemorrhoids. *("Na zdorovie" 's)*

(STANISLAVSKI pokes his head in.)

STANISLAVSKI. Nemirovich!

NEMIROVICH. Ladies and Gentlemen, in the theatre it is often said of people, "You are dispensable. If you do not perform well, you can be replaced." It has even been said, and not entirely in jest, that my job could be filled by a monkey with an abacus. The same could not possibly be said for my esteemed partner. So here, with an entertainment entirely of his own devising, sans abacus, is Konstantin Sergeievich Stanislavski.

(Enter STANISLAVSKI made up as a ludicrous parody of CHEKHOV.)

STANISLAVSKI. No applause. Please, I want no appreciation. By the way, I'd like to thank my sister for letting me smoke. I promise, Masha, no more than one. *(He takes out a huge cigar. Cough.)* You have been a great inspiration to me during your visit to my humble estate *(cough).* I planted all the acacias myself. In honor of this occasion, I've penned a new tragedy, uh comedy ... Now, rather than hand this play over to the Moscow Art Theatre to be violated by that imbecile, Stanislavski, I have decided to read selected scenes so their correct interpretation will not be a matter of dispute. Ladies and gentlemen, my latest play, *Uncle Cuckoo.* The play opens with no offstage sound effects.

CHEKHOV. *(stands)* Bravo! *(sits)*

STANISLAVSKI. Enter the country doctor and well-known writer Pavel Antonovich and his sister Marfa. Pavel studies his feet carefully and says, "The night is so still." *(MOSKVIN, LUZHKI, BUNIN and GORKY imitate cows, sheep, cuckoos, chickens, etc. STANISLAVSKI cuts them off.)* Marfa replies, "Would you like some tea?" End of Act I. At the beginning of Act II, the company of a famous Moscow theatre arrives at the doctor's estate in Yalta. Pavel Antonovich woos the actress Olgavina. Pavel speaks first: "Would you like to see my charts of foliage? *(From the listeners, scattered "No!" "Anything but that!" "Burn them!" etc. STANISLAVSKI reveals an easel on which there are charts.)* The first chart represents the area as it was fifty years ago. The small green tree-like objects represent trees. You'll notice that at the time there was an abundance of cattle in the district, and the entire vicinity was covered by a red grid. *(He flips th the second chart. There is one cow, no trees, and the grid has lost its horizontal lines.)* Now let us look at the area as it was twenty-five years ago. As you can see, the trees have entirely disappeared and the cow population has dwindled considerably.

MOSKVIN. What happened to the horizontal lines in the grid?

STANISLAVSKI. Due to the depletion of the forests they were used for kindling. And finally, the very same landscape as it appears today. *(He flips to third card: One dead cow.)* Everything is gone. The cow is dead. End of Act II. In Act III all the minor characters become involved in amorous triangles ... *(Pause. He begins to drop character and break down.)* ... in which everyone is making romantic overtures to everyone else ... *(Looks at NEMIROVICH and LILINA.)* ... except their respective spouses. *(Loses control completely.)* It's all too funny. I can't go on. *(Exits into the house. General applause.)*

BUNIN. What twilight melancholy!

LUZHKI. Bravo, Stanislavski!

MOSKVIN. What an actor!

GORKY. What a ham.

CHEKHOV. There you see? I told you I write comedies.

OLGA. Eat! Drink! Help yourselves, everyone.

MASHA. *(inebriated)* Yes! Listen to Olga; she's the mistress here now.

GORKY. When did Masha start drinking?

BUNIN. I've never seen her like this. *(CHEKHOV takes MASHA's drink away from her. She goes and pours another.)*

GORKY. Poor Masha. People can't adjust to change. I've seen it more and more lately. *(CHEKHOV and OLGA cross to GORKY and BUNIN.)* Anton, you know that old squire on the hill, Babyatkin?

CHEKHOV. Yes, I was called to his estate once to treat his gout.

GORKY. Did you know his land is being divided and parceled out to creditors? But what does he do? He stares out the window while workmen chop down his trees and plow up his gardens. They're carrying away his furniture while he smokes his Egyptian cigarettes and tells visitors his banker has everything under control.

CHEKHOV. What a shame. Babyatkin's gardens were the pride of Yalta.

GORKY. You see what I'm saying? When people ignore change it comes that much more quickly.

BUNIN. Leaving smoking craters of rotting corpses where once there were gardens.

OLGA. Maxim, if there is a revolution, what will happen to you?

BUNIN. Oh, he'll be all right. Minister of Culture for the new Peasant Tsar.

NEMIROVICH. And you, Ivan Alexeievich, what about you?

BUNIN. Oh, I'll be shot. Excuse me.

(STANISLAVSKI re-enters.)

NEMIROVICH. Luzhki, we're ready.

LUZHKI. Moskvin. *(LUZHKI and MOSKVIN exit.)*

MASHA. *(approaching BUNIN)* Ivan, I have to speak with you.

NEMIROVICH. Several months ago, we prevailed upon your dear sister to lend us a photograph of yourself. *(LUZHKI and MOSKVIN enter carrying a large painting covered by a protective cloth.)* From the brush of the great Sokovkin ... *(NEMIROVICH removes the cloth with a flourish. It is upside down. MOSKVIN and LUZHKI turn the portrait of CHEKHOV around.)*

CHEKHOV. It's so gloomy. *(Everyone is upset.)*

NEMIROVICH. Sokovkin is quite an admirer of yours.

STANISLAVSKI. He's seen every one of your plays.

LUZHKI. When he came backstage after *Vanya*, he was still crying.

CHEKHOV. I see. *(He turns and sees how devastated they are by his remark. He shakes his head, walks to his chair.)* Thank you, it's fine. Now I have something for you all.

LUZHKI. The play! The play! *(Everyone is excited. CHEK-HOV takes humidor, opens it, takes out medallions, and begins distributing them.)*

LUZHKI. *(disappointed)* Lockets?

(FYOKLA enters, goes to GORKY, whispers in his ear.)

GORKY. Where are they?

FYOKLA. Out front. *(He nods and follows her out.)*

LUZHKI. They're little books.

MOSKVIN. There's a seagull on the cover.

LUZHKI. And they're engraved: "To an actor who knows how to fill the stage." Lilina, what does yours say?

LILINA. "Your costumes are always fitting."

LUZHKI. Moskvin, read yours. *(MOSKVIN shakes his head. LUZHKI grabs it and reads.)* "A rare combination of humility and talent."

CHEKHOV. Read them later.

STANISLAVSKI. Wait, wait, everybody. Listen to this. "My plays would never be the same without you." *(Pleased, then realizes double meaning.)*

LUZHKI. Knipper's! Let's hear Knipper's!

OLGA. No, no.

EVERYONE. Read it, Knipper, read it!

OLGA. *(flustered)* I can't, it's too personal.

EVERYONE. Ahhh! *(Applause. MASHA laughs like a hyena. The members of the company thank CHEKHOV, some of them shaking his hand, etc. There is a long, anxious pause.)*

NEMIROVICH. Well, we'll certainly cherish these touching momentos, Anton Pavlovich. Now, before we leave your delightful villa, perhaps forever, is there anything else you'd like to tell us?

STANISLAVSKI. Or give us?

CHEKHOV. No, not really. *(Pause. Great disappointment. CHEKHOV looks at them, and makes a decision. He takes a leather-bound manuscript from under the cushion of his chair and holds it up.)* Take it, it's yours.

STANISLAVSKI. *The Three Siblings! (Both NEMIROVICH and STANISLAVSKI reach for it, check themselves, and walk away.)*

CHEKHOV. Well, it's here if you want it.

OLGA. *(raising glass)* Long life to *The Three Sisters!*

BUNIN. And to Anton Pavlovich! *("Na zdorovie" 's all around. GORKY staggers in, knocks painting off easel. He has a bloody nose and mouth.)*

NEMIROVICH. My God, it's Gorky!

BUNIN. Maxim! *(CHEKHOV moves to GORKY, starts to examine him.)*

STANISLAVSKI. A doctor. Someone get a doctor.

NEMIROVICH. *(Grabs STANISLAVSKI's arm.)* A doctor, Konstantin ... *(Indicates CHEKHOV.)*

STANISLAVSKI. Ah, yes, of course, a doctor. *(Realizes NEMIROVICH is touching him, pulls his arm away.)*

GORKY. It was the two from the cemetery, Anton. The simple gravediggers.

CHEKHOV. What did they do to you?

GORKY. Nothing, until I called the Tsar's mother a syphilitic slut.

BUNIN. You fool.

CHEKHOV. Nothing seems to be broken.

GORKY. He wrapped his shirt around the truncheon.

CHEKHOV. Don't talk. I only hope you're not bleeding internally. Masha, cold compresses. Fyokla, get my bag.

NEMIROVICH. I can't believe they'd go this far. And right on your doorstep, Anton.

CHEKHOV. There must have been some mistake.

GORKY. No mistake. They found the printing press, tortured the printer. He told them who wrote the leaflets. *(He touches his forehead and shows his bloody fingers to CHEKHOV.)* You see, Anton? It's real ...

CHEKHOV. Moskvin, Luzhki, gently ... To the sofa in the sitting room.

BUNIN. *(to GORKY)* Are you sure they weren't literary critics? *(GORKY starts to laugh, then clutches stomach in pain. MOSKVIN and LUZHKI carry GORKY into house. Everyone follows but NEMIROVICH. NEMIROVICH picks up the play. STANISLAVSKI reenters watching. NEMIROVICH offers him the script.)*

STANISLAVSKI. *(snatching the script)* You knew it, didn't you? *(pause)* You knew you could do as you liked, and the collaboration would continue. *(pause)* If I do this play with you, what kind of man will you think I am?

NEMIROVICH. A smart man. This production will allow

the Twentieth Century's most significant theatrical institution to survive another six months.

STANISLAVSKI. You've never had any difficulty separating business affairs and personal adventures, have you?

NEMIROVICH. None, whatsoever.

STANISLAVSKI. With me, if my diner doesn't digest well, I become an insufferable martinet at rehearsal.

NEMIROVICH. Why let something so trivial get in the way of your work?

STANISLAVSKI. We're not talking about a slice of tainted veal, are we?

NEMIROVICH. Ah, Kostya, for me, an interlude with a desirable woman is like a game of chance.

STANISLAVSKI. A toss of the dice, a spin of the wheel, a bet on a horse?

NEMIROVICH. Exactly.

STANISLAVSKI. Well, you shouldn't have taken the mare from my stable.

NEMIROVICH. Why don't we read the play together?

STANISLAVSKI. How was she with you? Did she moan with pleasure?

NEMIROVICH. Let's drop this.

NEMIROVICH. Did she dab perfume betwen her breasts? Did she call out your name?

NEMIROVICH. It's over.

STANISLAVSKI. How did she compare with the others? I suppose I'll learn what you taught her.

NEMIROVICH. Your capacity for melodrama is boundless.

STANISLAVSKI. Rivaled only by your cold-blooded

lechery. I came out here with the intention of killing you.

NEMIROVICH. Oh, really Konstantin.

STANISLAVSKI. Oh, yes, I did. A crime of passion. No court in Russia would ever convict me.

NEMIROVICH. What nonsense!

STANISLAVSKI. My God, did you share a brandy with her afterwards?

NEMIROVICH. Cognac. *(STANISLAVSKI pulls out a pistol.)* Wait. No! Don't shoot!

STANISLAVSKI. You are a coward, Nemirovich.

NEMIROVICH. I think under the circumstances I'm handling myself pretty well. What do you want?

STANISLAVSKI. I want to put a lead ball through your heart. No more petty disputes. No more cupity and deceit. No more budget limitations. The theatre will be all mine.

NEMIROVICH. Mother of God. Please help me!

STANISLAVSKI. Bastard! You'll burn in hell!

NEMIROVICH. No! *(STANISLAVSKI fires. NEMIROVICH falls, screams, twitches.)* I'm hit! I'm killed! What's this? *(Holds up wadding.)* A wad of cotton?

STANISLAVSKI. *(Heads to Up-Center door, turns.)* I may be a cuckold, but I'm also Russia's greatest living actor. *(He exits.)*

(BUNIN enters, followed by MOSKVIN, LUZHKI, and MASHA.)

LUZHKI. Good Lord!

MOSKVIN. What happened?

BUNIN. What's going on here? We heard a shot.

NEMIROVICH. Uh, uh .... nothing. Stanislavski was testing a pistol for our next production. Obviously the charge was too loud.

BUNIN. Obviously. That was bad timing, I'm afraid. After what happened to Gorky, everyone's a little jumpy.

LUZHKI. My heart leapt into my throat!

NEMIROVICH. How is Gorky?

(Boat whistle.)

NEMIROVICH. *(Looks at his watch.)* We have to be packed and on our way to the dock within the hour. Luzhki, Moskvin, make sure everything is ready. *(Exit NEMIRO-VICH, LUZHKI, and MOSKVIN. BUNIN pours himself a drink.)*

MASHA. *(fanning herself)* It's too hot for all this excitement.

BUNIN. Perhaps the rain will bring some relief. You wanted to talk?

MASHA. Yes. Would you pour me another one?

BUNIN. Are you sure?

MASHA. Yes. I like the rain. Papa liked the rain. During spring showers he used to sit under the veranda at our dacha in Melicovo like an emperor surveying his domain. He was so confident, so certain his seeds would sprout. Oh, why can't life be as predictable as nature?

BUNIN. It is. Or at least as unpredictable. A frost in June is like a sudden relapse of an old illness. An unexpected flood is like a revolution.

MASHA. I wish I had your brain, Ivan. A poet's mind. What a wonderful thing!

BUNIN. Wonderful, and utterly useless.

MASHA. Oh, wait, I just remembered, I have something for you. *(Runs out, comes back with shirt.)* It's been ready for two days.

BUNIN. *(Holds it up.)* Masha, it's good as new. Thank you.

MASHA. *(Throws her arms around BUNIN.)* Marry me, Ivan. Please marry me.

BUNIN. I do believe you've lost your mind.

MASHA. I'd make a perfect wife. You'll always have clean shirts. Your house will be well kept.

BUNIN. You've had too much to drink.

MASHA. I need you to love me.

BUNIN. Isn't there anything else I can do for you instead?

MASHA. Don't laugh at me. Who could manage your affairs better than I could?

BUNIN. There's one thing you're overlooking, Masha. I don't care for you.

MASHA. In time you could learn to like me. I wouldn't be any trouble.

BUNIN. You're not being very convincing about that.

MASHA. Ivan, don't deny yourself this happiness. Listen to me. I know I'm not good-looking.

BUNIN. Please, Masha, stop being so pathetic.

MASHA. *(dropping to her knees)* Try. You could love me, I know you could. *(BUNIN tries to exit, but she holds his leg.)* Can't you see how much I want you?

BUNIN. At least let's get away from the house. *(He drags her a few steps.)*

MASHA. You're my last chance.

BUNIN. *(Pulls out of his boot and backs off quickly.)* I'm sorry, I'm sorry. *(He exits.)*

MASHA. *(Throws his boot after him.)* Don't run away. What a fool I am! A drunken fool.

(CHEKHOV enters, smoking a cigar.)

CHEKHOV. *(calling into house)* He'll be all right. Just let him rest. What a day. *(MASHA takes CHEKHOV's cigar, throws it to the ground, and steps on it.)* Why did you do that?

MASHA. I have a bad habit of trying to stop you from killing yourself.

CHEKHOV. What harm can there be in one cigar?

MASHA. One more cigar, one more drink, one more night without sleep. I don't care. Do what you like. Marry your actress. She'll put you in a coffin quicker than anything you could do to yourself. I'm going to Moscow.

CHEKHOV. I think you should sober up first.

MASHA. I have to get away from Yalta now.

CHEKHOV. I need you here, Masha.

MASHA. You, Antosha, you forced me into this. You manipulated my life so that I've ended up with nothing. I just proposed to Bunin.

CHEKHOV. And?

MASHA. He fled in terror. You didn't have to use your influence this time.

CHEKHOV. When have I ever stopped you from doing anything?

MASHA. Fourteen years ago. Do you want the exact date? Alkexander, the bank clerk. He wanted to marry me.

CHEKHOV. I never said no.

MASHA. You delivered a silent ultimatum. If I had married him, a great chasm would have opened between us.

CHEKHOV. The choice was always yours. You merely showed some good sense. He would have gone with other women. You deserved a better man.

MASHA. Ha! If I had brought home the King of Spain, you would have said he wasn't good enough for me.

CHEKHOV. Stop lying to yourself. You've had a reasonably happy life.

MASHA. Happy? How can a person with no future be happy?

CHEKHOV. You're too upset to travel.

MASHA. You're going to marry her, aren't you?

CHEKHOV. I don't feel well.

MASHA. That won't work this time. My bags are already packed.

CHEKHOV. You packed your bags to go to Moscow, and then you spoke to Bunin about marriage?

MASHA. I knew it was hopeless. *(Starts to door. Stops.)* I'll stay if you want me to.

CHEKHOV. No, no, go on.

MASHA. Well, you do have Fyokla. *(She exits.)*

CHEKHOV. *(setting up the portrait)* I really don't feel well. *(looking at the painting)* But if I felt like he looks, I'd be dead.

(OLGA enters.)

OLGA. *(holding out locket)* What does this mean?

CHEKHOV. What it says.

OLGA. It's blank.

CHEKHOV. I was at a loss for words.

OLGA. Things can't stay the way they are, Anton, and silence won't change them.

CHEKHOV. I didn't say no.

OLGA. That simply won't do. *(taking CHEKHOV's hand and giving him the locket)* Thank you, Anton. We'll see each other in Moscow I'm sure. *(Starts to leave.)*

CHEKHOV. Olga.

OLGA. Please, there's no point in prolonging this.

CHEKHOV. I love you.

OLGA. Don't insult my intelligence.

CHEKHOV. It's true. In God's name, Olga, it's true.

OLGA. Then why not marry me?

CHEKHOV. Because I'm gravely ill. I know I've denied it and laughed it off, but that's a symptom of the disease. I'm a model consumptive. It was the same with my brother, Nikolai. To the end he pretended his ruddy cheeks were a sign of good health. I've had the bacillus for sixteen years.

OLGA. Impossible.

CHEKHOV. Yes, sixteen years.

OLGA. No!

CHEKHOV. It's invaded my intestines. The day before yesterday I passed blood.

OLGA. We'll go to the mountains. There's a new clinic there.

CHEKHOV. It's no use Olga. I'm dying.

OLGA. Patients sicker than yourself have recovered.

CHEKHOV. One in a thousand.

OLGA. That's good enough for me.

CHEKHOV. Oh, I do love you, Olga. In the last few days I've done nothing but stare into the abyss, and it's made me see how absurd it is to fear your love.

OLGA. I want you to live Anton Pavlovich Chekhov.

CHEKHOV. It's one thing for a doctor to watch his patients waste away, but when it's someone you love .... You can't know what it was like sitting by Nikolai's bedside those last months. My conscience will not allow you to suffer an experience like that.

OLGA. No matter what your conscience says, Anton, you want me to be with you, don't you?

CHEKHOV. Yes.

OLGA. I'll do anything for you. I'll make love to you. I'll bathe your forehead, I'll walk through hell with you, and if the worst should happen, I'll be with you when you die.

CHEKHOV. *(breaking down)* I'm afraid. I'm so afraid. *(OLGA cradles CHEKHOV in her arms.)* How futile! You make me yearn for a miracle. *(He holds up the locket.)* I'll have a wedding date engraved on this. *(They kiss.)* I promise you, by the end of the summer we'll be together.

(Enter STANISLAVSKI and MOSKVIN.)

STANISLAVSKI. At first glance it seems Vershinin is my part, but Toozenbach is actually the more interesting role.

MOSKVIN. Yes.

STANISLAVSKI. Yes, Toozenbach's the role for me. The

fire is exciting, isn't it? But why does it take place offstage? If we put it onstage, now that would be a challenge! *(Notices CHEKHOV.)* Anton, what would you think of putting the fire onstage?

CHEKHOV. That's an awful idea.

STANISLAVSKI. ust think of it. A packed house of theatregoers confronted with the spectacle of a roaring inferno.

CHEKHOV. No.

STANISLAVSKI. I think we could stage it so it would be quite safe.

CHEKHOV. Konstantin, don't you see? The fire is not the point of the scene.

STANISLAVSKI. Maybe we could work out a compromise.

CHEKHOV. No. *(He exits with OLGA.)*

(NEMIROVICH enters.)

NEMIROVICH. Moskvin, where's Luzhki?

MOSKVIN. I don't know.

NEMIROVICH. Well, find him. The carriages will arrive any minute now. *(MOSKVIN and NEMIROVICH exit.)*

(LILINA enters with suitcases.)

STANISLAVSKI. Lilina, the bags go out front. *(gently)* Never mind, I'll get them.

LILINA. Sit down, Kostya. I'm sorry I caused you so much pain.

STANISLAVSKI. Yes, you did. I hate you for it, and I don't

think I can ever forgive you.

LILINA. Oh, I think you will.

STANISLAVSKI. Why?

LILINA. Because for once I broke through your public armor and made you feel something.

STANISLAVSKI. How can you say that? I'm a very sensitive person.

LILINA. Yes, but you channel all your sensitivity into your work,

STANISLAVSKI. Do I?

LILINA. Yes. You shouldn't neglect the old Kostya. He's the only part of you that isn't acting.

STANISLAVSKI. *(He pulls her to him.)* No, you're right, you're right ... *(beat)* Lilina, would you mind terribly if I stopped sleeping in the study? *(LILINA holds him tighter.)* This is what we need, Lilina, more moments like these.

LILINA. Yes, Kostya.

STANISLAVSKI. *(distractedly)* No, no, the fire is *not* the point of the scene. It's only a reflection of the characters' inner turmoil. *(Realizes where he is.)* Ah! I'm sorry. Where were we? Oh, oh, I forgot my make-up kit. *(He runs into the house. LILINA picks up the suitcases, drops STANISLAVSKI's bag and exits with her own.)*

(LUZHKI and MOSKVIN enter.)

LUZHKI. I'm sorry, I'm sorry. I guess I dozed off.

(OLGA and NEMIROVICH enter.)

OLGA. Surprise, everybody. Masha is coming with us.

(STANISLAVSKI enters with make-up kit.)

NEMIROVICH. Everyone, hurry! Kostya, won't it be wonderful to get back to Moscow? We must have dinner at the new restaurant.
STANISLAVSKI. Huh! *(brusquely handing the play to NEM-IROVICH)* Here, draw up a budget for this.

(BUNIN, GORKY, MASHA and CHEKHOV enter. BUNIN is supporting GORKY.)

LUZHKI. Hey, look who's up and about.
BUNIN. He is risen.
GORKY. Take care, comrades. Never forget, Moscow is the belly of the beast.
MASHA. Antosha, promise me you'll get plenty of sleep.
CHEKHOV. Don't worry.
MASHA. There's fresh sausage hanging in the pantry. I laid in a good supply of tinned salmon. Fyokla has detailed instructions about your medicine. And don't work too hard.
NEMIROVICH. But do keep writing, old boy, and come to Moscow as soon as you can to help us with *The Three Sisters.*
STANISLAVSKI. But not if it will endanger your health in any way.

(LILINA enters.)

BUNIN. Good-bye, Masha.

MASHA. Good-bye. *(She exits.)*

NEMIROVICH. Enough. It's late.

EVERYONE. Good-bye, thank you, *(etc.)*

CHEKHOV. Oh, Moskvin.

MOSKVIN. Yes.

CHEKHOV. Remember, I wrote the part of Toozenbach for you. *(STANISLAVSKI chokes. MOSKVIN and LUZHKI exit. LILINA points at suitcase and leaves. STANISLAVSKI picks it up and follows. OLGA crosses to CHEKHOV. He takes her hand.)* I'll envy the rat that lives below the floor of your theatre. *(OLGA and CHEKHOV embrace.)*

NEMIROVICH. Olga, the carriages are leaving. *(OLGA turns and raises hand in farewell festure. CHEKHOV responds by holding up locket. OLGA exits.)* Good-bye, Anton Pavlovich, *(indicating play)* ... and thank you, thank you very much.

CHEKHOV. You're welcome, Vladimir Ivanovich. But next time you're on tour, do what Stanislavski did — take a tumble with the maid. *(NEMIROVICH exits bewildered.)*

BUNIN. Well, goodnight, Anton.

CHEKHOV. Goodnight, Ivan. Gorky, you should be sleeping.

GORKY. I'll sleep when I'm dead. *(BUNIN and GORKY exit. CHEKHOV sits on bench.)*

(FYOKLA enters with suitcase. She is dressed to travel. She approaches CHEKHOV but he does not see her. Offstage the carriages are heard reining up. FYOKLA exits silently. A few seconds

later we hear the sound of the carriage leaving. Pause.)

CHEKHOV. They're gone. Now maybe I can have some peace. So, *The Three Sisters* are on their way to Moscow. If I could only go with them. I can see rehearsals, now. He'll have the whole cast snapping twigs to simulate the sound of the fire. *(laughs)* Oh, Knipper, what hast thou wrought? Chekhov married at this point in his life?

(faint thunder)

CHEKHOV. In a hundred years, all this might be washed into the sea.

(big clap of thunder)

CHEKHOV. Maybe sooner. Hmm, Babyatkin's gardens. Fyokla! Bring my notebook. Let it rain! It's life that matters not vapid stories and silly vaudevilles. *(coughing fit)*

(crash of thunder)

CHEKHOV. *(crying to the heavens)* Nikolai! *(to himself)* If only I have time? Why? Why did I wait so long? I'm living my life in reverse. A lovestruck schoolboy at death's door, an optimist with lungs full of blood. *(He lights a cigar.)*

(The rain begins. Big drops hit the ground, and one puts out the cigar.)

CHEKHOV. *(Starts to house, covers the portrait with the protective cloth, thinks, and then uncovers it. He exits into the house.)* **Fyokla!**

(Lights fade.)

END OF ACT II

COSTUME PLOT

ACT I, SCENE 1

FYOKLA:
- Skirt
- Bodice
- Blouse
- Apron
- Stockings
- Bloomers
- Scarf
- Boots

CHEKHOV:
- Double-breasted jacket
- Shirt
- Trousers
- Suspenders
- Vest
- Tie
- Socks
- Slippers
- Pinc-nez eyeglasses
- Pocket watch
- Hat

BUNIN:
- Hunting jacket

Shirt
Riding breeches
Riding boots
Tie
Belt
Socks
Gloves

GORKY:
Peasant shirt
Peasant pants
Russian boots
Wide belt
Cap

MASHA:
Blouse
Skirt
Belt
Corset
Petticoat
Apron
Stockings
Shoes

OLGA KNIPPER:
Blouse
2-piece travelling suit
Corset
Petticoats
Stockings

Shoes
Garters
Hat
Gloves
Earrings
Brooch
Purse

NEMIROVICH-DANCHENKO:
2-piece suit
Pique vest
Shirt
Tie
Suspenders
Straw hat
Walking stick
Pocket watch with chain
Shoes
Socks
Rings
Cufflinks

ACT I, SCENE 2
OLGA KNIPPER:
Evening dress
Petticoat
Corset
Stockings
Pumps
Necklace
Earrings
Shawl

MOSKVIN:
- Jacket
- Shirt
- Vest
- Trousers
- Tie
- Shoes
- Socks
- Suspenders

LUZHKI:
- Jacket
- Shirt
- Vest
- Trousers
- Tie
- Shoes
- Socks
- Suspenders

BUNIN:
- Evening jacket
- Evening trousers
- Evening vest
- Formal shirt
- Formal tie
- Evening pumps
- Socks
- Shirt studs
- Cufflinks
- Gloves

GORKY:
>   Red silk Russian shirt
>   Russian trousers
>   Wide belt with ornate buckle
>   Russian boots

MASHA:
>   Evening dress
>   Petticoat
>   Corset
>   Cameo
>   Earrings
>   Stockings
>   Pumps

NEMIROVICH-DANCHENKO:
>   Evening jacket
>   Evening trousers
>   Evening vest
>   Formal shirt
>   Formal tie
>   Evening pumps
>   Socks
>   Shirt studs
>   Cufflinks
>   Gloves

LILINA:
>   Evening dress
>   Petticoat
>   Corset

Stockings
Pumps
Necklace
Earrings
Kimono robe
Nightgown
Slippers
Wedding band

CHEKHOV:
Double-breasted jacket
Matching trousers
Shirt
Tie
Shoes
Socks
Suspenders
Pinc-nez glasses

STANISLAVSKI:
Velvet jacket
Velvet vest
Plaid trousers
Bow tie
Shirt
Suspenders
Shoes
Socks
Cape
Hat
Cufflinks

Gloves
Duplicate trousers with mudstains

FYOKLA:
Same as Scene 1

ACT II
OLGA:
2-piece travelling suit
Silk blouse
Corset
Petticoat
Stockings
Boots
Hat
Gloves
Earrings
Purse

FYOKLA:
Same as Act I, Scene 1
Add:
Coat
Hat

LUZHKI:
Same as Act I, Scene 2

MOSKVIN:
Same as Act I, Scene 2

CHEKHOV:
   Same as Act I, Scene 1

BUNIN:
   Same as Act I, Scene 1

GORKY:
   Same as Act I, Scene 1

MASHA:
   Skirt *(same as Act I, Scene 1)*
   Fancy blouse
   Crochet vest
   Hat
   Petticoat
   Corset
   Stockings
   Shoes
   Add:
      Jacket
      Gloves
      Purse

NEMIROVICH:
   Same as Act I, Scene 1

LILINA:
   Blouse
   Skirt
   Corset
   Petticoat

Stockings
Shoes
Necklace
Earrings
Add:
    Duster coat
    Hat with veil
    Purse
    Gloves

STANISLAVSKI:
    Light-colored 2-piece suit
    Shirt
    Tie
    Belt
    Shoes
    Socks
    Straw hat
    Gloves
    Add for costume:
        Pince-nez
        Chekhov's hat
        Chekhov's double-breasted suit jacket

PROPERTY PLOT

ONSTAGE PRESET (PRESHOW)
>2 wicker armchairs
>1 small end table with ashtray
>1 wooden bench
>1 table on lower porch for samovar
>1 ottoman

>Interior rooms should look furnished and have drapes on all doors and windows.

>There should be clay pots of geraniums set around upper and lower porch.

ONSTAGE PRESET (ACT II)
>1 large table covered with lace table cloth
>On top:
>>10 plates
>>10 napkins
>>10 sets of silverware
>>Assorted glasses

OFFSTAGE PRESET
Upstage Center
For FYOKLA:
>1 samovar with teapot on top

1 large silver tray with:
Creamer,
Sugar bowl,   Tongs,
4 clear glass cups and saucers,
4 teaspoons,
4 cloth napkins
1 white cleaning cloth
1 plate with rolls
1 plate with sandwiches
1 fly rod with reel
1 tray of oysters
1 mason jar of tea with cloth cover tied on
1 wooden cigar humidor with cigars inside
1 silver holder containing wooden matches
1 tray with glasses
1 tray of hors d'oeuvres
1 linen table cloth
1 tray of food
1 manuscript of "The Three Sisters"
1 suitcase
1 locket box filled with six (6) lockets

For GORKY:
1 bottle of French Beaujolais

For NEMIROVICH:
1 bottle of vodka
1 wadding from pistol

For LUZHKI:
1 gramophone
2 matched suitcases

For LILINA:
    1 needlepoint
    1 needle
    1 thread
    1 sewing basket
    1 make-up kit containing:
       Standing mirror, Nose putty, Clown white,
       Spirit gum, Assorted brushes, Face powder
       Dry rouge, Assorted make-up tubes, Sponges,
       Towel

For BUNIN:
    10 rubles
    1 wrapped package containing framed photo of
    Tolstoy

For MASHA:
    1 tray of eight champagne bottles
    1 "repaired" shirt

For STANISLAVSKI:
    1 pistol
    3 cigars for coat pocket

For CHEKHOV:
    1 cigar

Offstage Right
For Chekhov:
    1 medical bag
    1 small leather notebook

1 wooden pencil
1 string of trout
Matches for his pocket

For OLGA:
1 Chekhov's hat

For FYOKLA:
1 Chekhov's fly rod with reel

For GORKY:
1 fly rod with reel

For BUNIN:
1 fly rod with reel

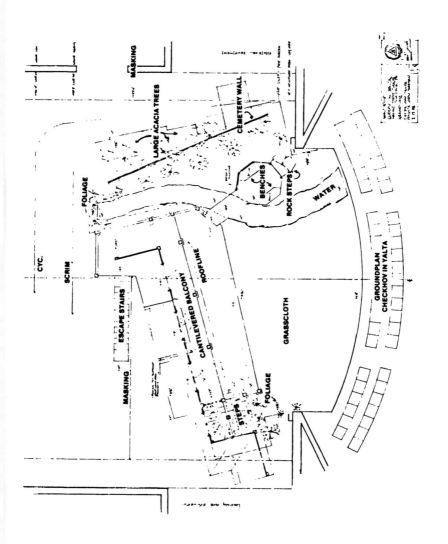

GROUNDPLAN
CHECKHOV IN YALTA

MASKING

LARGE ACACIA TREES

CEMETERY WALL

FOLIAGE

BENCHES

ROCK STEPS

WATER

CYC.

SCRIM

ESCAPE STAIRS

MASKING

CANTILEVERED BALCONY

ROOFLINE

GRASSCLOTH

STEPS

FOLIAGE

JOHN DRIVER

. . . is a member of seven show business unions: AEA, AFTRA, DG, DGA, SAG, SSD&C, and WGA. He was director, co-author and original cast member of the long-running hit *SCRAMBLED FEET. SHAKESPEARE'S CABARET, which John directed on Broadway at the Bijou Theatre earned a Tony nomination. He has video directed five award-winning productions from Minneapolis Children's Theatre Company, which can currently be seen on HBO. John's Broadway acting career began as one of the early GREASE greasers, and then led to the role of Bill in OVER HERE!, a part which earned him the Theatre World Award. From television he was familiar to millions of viewers as Kevin on THE EDGE OF THE NIGHT. As a writer John has completed the book and lyrics for LISA AND DAVID, a Broadway-bound dramatic musical. CHEKHOV IN YALTA, which he co-authored, won the Los Angeles Drama Critics Award for Best Play of 1981.

JEFFREY HADDOW

. . . was co-author and member of the original cast of *SCRAMBLED FEET, the musical revue that ran two years at the Village Gate. His play, THIN ICE was also presented Off-Broadway at the WPA Theatre. With his wife Maya, he translated and adapted a contemporary Polish play, VALESA, which was published in Yale's "Theatre" magazine, and, like CHEKHOV IN YALTA, had its world premiere at the Mark Taper in Los Angeles. In addition to his theatre work, Mr. Haddow has also written numerous screenplays and teleplays. He is a graduate of Northwestern University and lives in Manhattan.

THE SCENE
Theresa Rebeck

Little Theatre / Drama / 2m, 2f / Interior Unit Set
A young social climber leads an actor into an extra-marital affair, from which he then creates a full-on downward spiral into alcoholism and bummery. His wife runs off with his best friend, his girlfriend leaves, and he's left with… nothing.

"Ms. Rebeck's dark-hued morality tale contains enough fresh insights into the cultural landscape to freshen what is essentially a classic boy-meets-bad-girl story."
- *New York Times*

"Rebeck's wickedly scathing observations about the sort of self-obsessed New Yorkers who pursue their own interests at the cost of their morality and loyalty."
- *New York Post*

"The Scene is utterly delightful in its comedic performances, and its slowly unraveling plot is thought-provoking and gut-wrenching."
- *Show Business Weekly*

Breinigsville, PA USA
08 February 2010
232072BV00005B/7/P